UK MET
LIGHT RAIL SYSTEMS
INCLUDING LONDON UNDERGROUND

FIRST EDITION

Robert Pritchard & Alan Yearsley

Published by Platform 5 Publishing Ltd,
52 Broadfield Road, Sheffield, S8 0XJ, England.

Printed in England by The Lavenham Press Ltd, Lavenham, Suffolk.

ISBN 978 1 909431 37 9

▲ Although known as the "Underground", around 55% the London Underground network is actually above ground. On 21 April 2016 a train of S8 Stock crosses the Grand Union Canal with a service from Watford to Aldgate. This section of line will close when the extension of the Metropolitan Line to Croxley and Watford Junction opens.

David Palmer

CONTENTS

Front Cover Photograph: At Neasden Jubilee Line and Metropolitan Line trains can be seen side-by-side. On 5 July 2016 Jubilee Line 1996 Stock 96040/96015 is leaving the station for Stanmore as S8 Stock 21112/111 passes through for Uxbridge. **Robert Pritchard**

Back Cover Photograph (top): Tyne & Wear Metro 4019+4045 arrive at Newcastle Airport with a late afternoon service from South Hylton on 13 August 2016. **Robert Pritchard**

Back Cover Photograph (bottom): Manchester Metrolink 3063 leaves Piccadilly Gardens for Piccadilly on 16 February 2016. **Robert Pritchard**

FOREWORD TO THE FIRST EDITION

Welcome to the first edition of this new Platform 5 guide to the rolling stock of the UK's metro and light rail systems. For many years basic fleet details of the UK's light railway systems have been listed in the annual Platform 5 publication "British Railways Locomotives and Coaching Stock". These listings have never been entirely satisfactory in terms of the level of detail provided, nor did they fall within the specific remit of that publication.

Therefore we have taken the opportunity to enhance these listings in this new publication and for the first time provide a detailed listing of the rolling stock of London Underground Limited. A larger page size has been adopted to enable better use of photographic illustrations and a completely new set of maps have been specially commissioned for this publication.

Also included are preserved vehicles originally built or having worked on the main systems, although the relatively recent construction of several UK light rail networks means several of the present systems have yet to see any vehicles move into preservation. As well as passenger carrying vehicles, details of the engineers' fleets and on-track machines are also included.

Our aim has been to provide a comprehensive guide to the fleets, including not just fleet lists but also an overview of operations on each system and other useful information including brief history, route details, service frequencies and fare details for each system.

We hope you will find the book a useful source of reference and a valuable addition to your collection.

ACKNOWLEDGEMENTS & CONTACT DETAILS

Thanks are given to all the individuals and organisations who have helped in the compilation of this book. Special thanks go to Peter Hall, particularly for his work in tracking down preserved stock and guiding us through the area of On-Track Machines. Special thanks also go to Trackmaps for its cartography.

The authors would welcome updates and corrections to this book, of which readers have first-hand knowledge. Please send any notifications to Robert Pritchard at the Platform 5 address on the title page, or by email to updates@platform5.com (Tel 0114 255 2625).

This book is updated to information received by May 2017.

UPDATES

Updates to Platform 5 UK handbooks can be found in the monthly magazine **Today's Railways UK**, which is the only UK railway magazine to publish official Platform 5 stock changes. **Today's Railways UK** is available from all good newsagents or on post-free direct subscription. Please see the inside cover of this book for further details.

INTRODUCTION

This book lists the passenger-carrying vehicles of all ten public-carrier light rail and metro systems in the UK. Locomotives and on-track machines that fall within the custodianship of each system and are permitted to operate under their own power or in train formations throughout those systems are also included.

Locomotives, road-rail vehicles and other maintenance machines normally only permitted to be used within depot confines or within engineering possessions are not included, nor are contractors' locomotives and on-track machines that may see use on the networks for short periods.

Vehicles that previously saw service on the currently active networks but are now considered to be preserved are included. Historic tramway vehicles that still exist but spent their working lives on now-closed tramways in the UK are not included.

GENERAL NOTES

This book has been divided into three main sections covering The London Underground, Preserved Underground Stock and UK Light Rail and Metro Systems. Within the London Underground section, each line has its own sub-section; these are listed broadly in chronological order of age of rolling stock used on each line, with tube lines preceding Sub-Surface lines.

For every LU line in section 1 and light rail undertaking in section 3, a general introduction provides a brief history of each line and details of day-to-day operations including service frequencies, operating times and depot/maintenance information. Further details of fares and ticketing requirements are also provided and where appropriate future plans for each line or network.

This introduction is followed by detailed fleet lists with tabulated technical data and unit formations where appropriate. Detailed technical specifications should be read with reference to the following notes and also the appendices at the back of the book.

NUMBERS AND NAMES

There is no universal numbering scheme in place for UK metros and light rail systems, each system instead adopting their own numbering scheme. Vehicles are listed within each sub-section in chronological order of current running number. Notes regarding individual numbering schemes are provided within each sub-section as appropriate. Former numbers carried by preserved vehicles are shown. The current name of vehicles, where carried, is shown.

LOCATIONS

Details of the depots used for routine servicing and maintenance are provided in the introduction to each sub-section; depot allocations are not in use. For preserved items the location at which the item can usually be found is given, although it should be noted that some vehicles, especially locomotives, sometimes visit other locations for operation, display or mechanical attention. A list of locations with OS grid references can be found in Appendix I: List of Locations.

WHEEL ARRANGEMENT

For modern metro and light rail vehicles (and main line diesel and electric locomotives) the system whereby the number of powered wheels on a bogie is denoted by a letter (A = 1, B = 2, C = 3 etc) and the number of unpowered axles is denoted by a number is used. The letter "o" after a letter indicates that each axle is individually powered and a + symbol indicates that the bogies are intercoupled.

The Whyte notation is used for steam locomotives and diesel shunting locomotives with coupled driving wheels. The number of leading wheels are given, followed by the number of driving wheels, then the number of trailing wheels. Suffixes are used to denote tank locomotives as follows: T = side tank, PT = pannier tank, ST = saddle tank, WT = well tank. For example 2-6-2T. 4w indicates a four-wheeled non-bogied vehicle.

DIMENSIONS

The units of measure used in this book are those most appropriate to current usage. In most cases this is the metric system except where the imperial system is still in common use. For example, length, height and width dimensions are usually given in metric metres, but maximum speed is given in imperial miles per hour. In most instances weights are stated in metric tonnes, except in the case of a few very old vehicles where imperial tons are used.

Steam locomotive cylinder dimension are given in imperial feet and inches; the diameter is given first, followed by the stroke. (I) indicates two inside cylinders, (O) two outside cylinders.

ACCOMMODATION

The number of seats in each vehicle is given. First Class accommodation is not provided in any vehicles listed in this book so all seats can be regarded as a single classification.

BUILD DETAILS

For each vehicle the builder and year of construction are given. A full list of builders can be found in Appendix IV: Private Manufacturers.

▲ Northern Line 51706/532 arrives at the wide platforms of Euston station (Bank branch) with a service for Morden on 11 June 2016. **Robert Pritchard**

1. LONDON UNDERGROUND

INTRODUCTION

The London Underground is the world's oldest metro system covering a total of 11 lines, with a history going back to 1863 when the Metropolitan Railway opened its first stretch of line between Paddington and Farringdon. Much of the rest of the sub-surface network also dates from between the 1860s and the early 20th century, and the first deep level tube line opened in 1890 between Stockwell and King William Street on what is now the Northern Line. The largest metro system in Europe, today London Underground serves a total of 270 stations and covers 402 km (250 miles) of track.

In total there are 11 Underground lines, each shown in their own colour on the official map. Four lines, the Circle, District, Hammersmith & City and Metropolitan are Sub-Surface Lines (SSLs), since they operate above ground or just below ground and use trains built to the same loading gauge as rolling stock on the National Rail network (with which they share tracks in a number of locations). The other seven Underground lines (Bakerloo, Piccadilly, Central, Waterloo & City, Northern, Jubilee and Victoria) are deep level tube lines running in tunnels bored rather than built by the "cut and cover" method used for sub-surface tunnels. The "cut and cover" method caused a great deal of surface disruption during construction so towards the end of the 19th century a new system of tunnelling was developed that involved boring a circular tunnel at deep level and lining it with cast iron segments. Lines built in this way have a separate tunnel for each direction of running and because of the small diameter it is only possible to accommodate trains of very restricted dimension – the Tube stock. Most of the deep level tube lines do also include some above ground sections in the suburbs, however, although the entire LU network is often colloquially referred to as "The Tube". Despite its name, only 45% of the network is in tunnels. This section contains separate more detailed histories and descriptions of each line.

London's underground railway system developed rather haphazardly, creating traffic as it grew without any central control or planning, except that nominally exercised by Parliament, for almost 70 years until the formation of the London Passenger Transport Board (LPTB) in 1933 (although the brand name Underground first started to be displayed at station entrances in 1908). As a result of this the various lines appeared to have little in common apart from the standard track gauge of 1435 mm: there were different tunnel sizes, different platform lengths, different types of signalling and even different current rail systems. All these variations gave rise to different types of rolling stock. Within the limits of cost and time, considerable standardisation has been achieved, as the new S Stock on the Sub-Surface lines and 1995/1996 Tube stocks on the Northern and Jubilee lines show. The forthcoming New Tube For London for the deep tube lines will allow further standardisation.

Subsequent political changes saw LPTB evolve through the London Transport Executive (LTE) in 1948, London Transport Board (LTB) in 1963, London Regional Transport (LRT) in 1984, and now London Underground Ltd (LU), part of Transport for London (TfL) which was formed in 2000 when the Greater London Authority was established along with the directly elected Mayor of London who is responsible for all forms of public transport (apart from most National Rail services). The terms London Transport and London Underground were commonly used for all these organisations, and LT and LU are used interchangeably within this book.

THE TRAIN FLEET

London Underground operates seven basic train types, each line generally operating a different type of train (the exceptions being 1992 Stock of a similar type used on both the Central and Waterloo & City lines and the S Stock universally used on all the Sub-Surface Lines).

Official LU rolling stock designation is by the year in which manufacture started for Tube stock, and by arbitrary letter with year suffix for Sub-Surface stock, e.g. the Central Line's 1992 tube stock is abbreviated to 92TS. Naturally there are exceptions to every rule – 1995 and 1996 Tube Stock entered service the opposite way around, while S Stock is referred to as S7 or S8, denoting the number of cars in the train, not the year of manufacture.

Tube stock is built to a much lower overall height than Sub-Surface stock to fit the more restricted loading gauge of the deep level tunnels. The height of Tube stock varies between 2.869 m for 1992 Stock used on the Central and Waterloo & City Lines and 2.888 m for Piccadilly Line 1973 Stock (see individual entries for details) to fit the differing sizes of tunnels built by different railway companies. The now withdrawn D78 Stock had a height of 3.630 m, and the height of S7 and S8 Stock vehicles is 3.682 m.

Despite the long period of central control and deployment of large successive standardised fleets such as 1920s "Standard" stock, 1938 Stock, and 1959/1962 Stock common to several lines, today's situation is largely reversed with dedicated captive fleets on each line. The notable exception is the S Stock now common to all four Sub-Surface lines (although 8-car sets are limited to the Metropolitan Line with 7-cars used on the other three SSLs).

In this book rolling stock is listed chronologically by the official designation of all types. Therefore the order is 1972, 1973, 1992, 1995, 1996, 2009 and S8/S7. All 1967 and D78 Stock has now been withdrawn from fleet service. Some 1967 vehicles were initially stored at Eastleigh Works but were being scrapped at the time of going to press.

In January 2016 TfL issued an Invitation to Tender for the NTFL fleet, with the contract expected to be awarded in autumn 2017. A total of 250 new trains are to be built, the first 100 of which are due to enter service on the Piccadilly Line from 2023. A further 100 trains are envisaged for the Central Line, 40 for the Bakerloo Line and ten for the Waterloo & City Line, with entry into service due for completion by 2033. The NFTL trains will be the first trains on the deep level tube lines to feature air conditioning and walk-through gangways, and will be capable of driverless automatic operation.

Most present stock types have two thirds-to-three quarters of axles motored within a full train, but 1992 and S Stocks have all axles motored. 1972, 1973 and 1992 Stock have traditional series-wound Direct Current (DC) commutator traction motors and the newer 1995, 1996, 2009 and S Stocks, three-phase Alternating Current (AC) synchronous motors. 1972 and 1973 traction motors are nose-suspended while 1992, 1995, 1996, 2009 and S Stocks have bogie-mounted motors and flexible drives via a gearbox. 1972 and 1973 Stocks have conventional camshaft resistance controls, 1992 chopper, 1996 GTO, and 1995, 2009 and S Stock are IGBT.

▲ This view at Neasden on 5 July 2016 clearly shows the different gauge between Tube stock 96034/093 (Jubilee Line 1996 Stock) and Metropolitan Line Sub-Surface S8 Stock 21094/093. **Robert Pritchard**

Again, despite much standardisation over many years, successive developments in train protection systems have also influenced the trend towards line specific captive stock fleets. All LU trains are equipped with automatic train protection and have been for many years. Train borne tripcocks and track side train stops form the traditional system and are still in use on the Bakerloo, Piccadilly and all Sub-Surface Lines. The then new Victoria Line opened in 1967 with a unique LT developed system. Central, Jubilee and Northern lines followed in the 21st Century and the original Victoria line system has now been replaced. Each line specific train protection system is listed.

Unlike on the National Rail network, LU stock is not generally formed of fixed formation trains, the exception being the new 2009 and S Stock, plus the Northern Line 1995 Stock which is now generally used in fixed formations. Units are generally formed of motor and trailer cars semi-permanently coupled. Units, even those in fixed formations, do not have set numbers, unlike on the national network, although they are sometimes referred to as "Train 1" etc.

All trains currently in service have bar couplers between cars and LU automatic Wedgelock between units, except S Stock which have flange muff couplers between cars. In addition S Stock auto couplers have pneumatic connections.

Automatic Train Operation (ATO), whereby the train effectively drives itself and the driver simply opens and closes the doors and presses a start button, is currently in use on the Central, Jubilee, Northern and Victoria Lines (the Victoria Line having used this method of operation since its opening). ATO is planned to be extended to the Circle and Hammersmith & City Lines in spring 2018, and later to the District and Metropolitan Lines. The Bakerloo, Piccadilly and Waterloo & City Line trains continue to be driven manually, and this is expected to be the case until the introduction of NTFL trains on these lines.

Maximum speed quoted is the line limit; the stock may well have a higher design speed.

All LUL passenger trains are electrically powered vehicles which are driven on truck-mounted motors. Not all cars have motors and some are purely for carrying passengers. These unmotored cars are termed "trailers". The following Type Codes are used throughout the book:

DM	Driving Motor = powered car with driving cab;
NDM	Non Driving Motor = powered car without driving controls; see also;
M	Non Driving Motor
M1	Non Driving Motor 1st variant (S Stock);
M2	Non Driving Motor 2nd variant (S Stock);
MS	Non-Driving Motor fitted with Sandite equipment (S Stock);
T	Trailer = unpowered car without driving controls;
UNDM	Uncoupling Non Driving Motor = powered car with shunting driving control.

De-icing cars are marked with a blue circle next to the number and these are listed in this publication. When actually de-icing a small blue external light is lit.

All passenger carrying LU trains carry a standard livery. This is principally white, with a wide blue lower bodyside band, a red front end and red doors.

In photo captions in the LU section of this book the full train formations are given where known, listed by the lowest fleet number of that set/half set/quarter set.

▲ Traditional LU traction supply is a nominal 630 V DC although some lines are being upgraded to 750 V DC, the traditional voltage used on the National Rail third rail network. On 15 June 2016 S8 Stock 21060/059 picks up current at Rayners Lane. **Robert Pritchard**

TRACTION SUPPLY

Traditional LU traction supply is a nominal 630 V DC from third and fourth rail – but upgrading to 750 V DC is taking place on some lines, dependent on the ability of newer trains to accept the higher voltage. Voltage on parts of the Metropolitan Line and the Hammersmith & City line between Hammersmith and Paddington has already been increased to 750 V DC. It is eventually intended to convert the whole network to the higher voltage.

The current is collected by the trains from two conductor rails laid on each track in addition to the running rails, known as a four-rail DC system. The conductor rails are insulated from earth by porcelain "pots" mounted on the sleepers. Where points or crossings occur in the running rails, gaps are left in the current rails to allow the train wheels to pass freely through the junction and to ensure the shoegear of trains using the conflicting route does not foul it.

MAINTENANCE

Almost all maintenance work on LU trains is carried out at depots, but individual components such as motors, motor alternators, compressors and wheelsets units may be sent away for major overhaul, either to the Railway Engineering Works (REW) at Acton or to outside contractors.

The transfer of heavy overhaul work to the maintenance depots has changed the type of work undertaken at Acton. Instead of carrying out heavy overhauls most of the work is now repairing and overhauling components sent by road from the depots.

It should be noted that the 1995 and 1996 Tube stocks have a different ownership and maintenance regime to the rest of the LU fleet. The 1995 Stock is owned by HSBC/RBS or Alstom and leased to LU. The trains manufacturers, Alstom, has a contract to maintain the trains at Morden and Golders Green. The 1996 Stock is owned by London Underground but a maintenance contract is in place with Alstom to maintain the trains at Stratford Market depot.

Finally, the depot at Ruislip is Transplant Rail Operations engineering train base depot.

▲ A Central Line 1992 Stock set undergoes overhaul at its home depot at Ruislip on 9 December 2015. **Keith Fender**

PASSENGER NUMBERS

The most recent line by line annual passenger figures available at the time of going to press are for 2011–12:

Central Line: 260.9 million
Northern Line: 252.3 million
Piccadilly Line: 210.2 million
District Line: 208.3 million
Victoria Line: 200 million
Circle and Hammersmith & City: 114.6 million
Bakerloo Line: 111.1 million
Metropolitan Line: 66.7 million
Waterloo & City Line: 15.9 million

Total: 1178.3 million (2011–12). In 2015–16 the total had increased to 1349.3 million. (Note: There may be discrepancies between the line by line figures and the total due to rounding.)

TICKETING AND FARES

The LU and National Rail networks within Greater London are divided into nine fare zones, and fares are calculated according to the number of zones through which the passenger travels. When making just one or two single journeys on the Underground in a day, the best value fares can be obtained by tapping a TfL "Oyster card" smartcard or a contactless credit or debit card on the ticket gate or card reader at the station entrance before boarding and at the exit after alighting. Ordinary paper tickets are still available for a single journey, but are much more expensive than when using an Oyster card or contactless payment card. In 2017 a single journey within Zone 1 costs £2.40 with an Oyster or contactless card, or £4.90 with a paper ticket.

In recent years most ticket offices have been closed at LU stations. Oyster cards can be obtained from ticket machines at stations, TfL Visitor Centres at key stations in central London, newsagents and convenience stores displaying the "Oyster Ticket Stop" sign, or ordered online via the TfL website. Many passengers increasingly may prefer to use a contactless bank card, as fare payments will still be processed in exactly the same way as with an Oyster card provided that the same card is used to touch in and touch out on the same journey. Oyster cards can be topped up at ticket machines at stations and at Oyster Ticket Stop shops. They will only work if the card holder has enough credit on the card for the journey being made.

Visitors to London can buy a Visitor Oyster card in advance before travelling to London. These cost £3 and come pre-loaded with an amount of credit of the user's choice between £10 and £50. They work in the same way as an ordinary Oyster card.

Paper One Day Travelcards are also still available, and are recommended for exploring London, especially if you plan to spend any length of time on stations observing trains, as journeys using Oyster or contactless cards are subject to a time limit, and the maximum fare will be charged if you exceed this limit or forget to touch out at the end of the journey. However, unfortunately paper Zones 1–2 and off-peak Zones 1–4 Travelcards have now been abolished, so only the Zones 1–6 version is still offered (plus an Anytime version for Zones 1–4). In 2017 the Zones 1–6 Travelcard costs £12.30 off-peak (or Zones 1–4 Anytime) and the Anytime Zones 1–6 version costs £17.50. There are also versions available for Zones 1–7, 1–8 and 1–9.

If you do choose to use an Oyster or contactless card for several journeys on the same day, you will receive an automatic price cap once you have used a certain amount of credit; in most cases this is the same as, or slightly less than, the cost of an equivalent One Day Travelcard for the journeys that you have made. Zones 1–2 and 1–4 price caps do still apply despite the withdrawal of paper Travelcards covering only these zones.

A paper Travelcard bought on a Friday is valid on Night Tube services until 04.30 on the Saturday, and similarly one purchased on a Saturday will be valid on Night Tube services until 04.30 on the Sunday.

Paper Travelcards, Oyster and contactless cards are also valid on all other forms of public transport in Greater London: buses, National Rail services, London Overground, the Docklands Light Railway, and London Tramlink.

Greater London residents are entitled to a 60+ Oyster Photocard when aged 60–65 or a Freedom Pass when aged 66 or over (or disabled). Both of these passes allow free travel on the Underground, buses, DLR, Tramlink and London Overground at all times (Freedom Passes are also valid on National Rail services outside the morning peak period). Pensioners and disabled people from other parts of England (but not from Scotland, Wales or Northern Ireland) may use their concessionary travel passes for free travel on London buses, but NOT on the Underground or any other modes of transport in London.

Full details of fares and tickets available can be found on the TfL website (www.tfl.gov.uk) and on the independent Oyster Rail site: www.oyster-rail.org.uk.

PHOTOGRAPHY

Photography and filming is permitted on LU stations and trains provided that you are doing so only for non-commercial purposes. However, for safety reasons flash photography and the use of tripods are prohibited under Section 4.5 of the TfL Conditions of Carriage (see http://content.tfl.gov.uk/tfl-conditions-of-carriage.pdf). Photography and filming permits are available from the LU Film Unit at £50 per month for commercial photographers.

There have been occasional reports of station staff wrongly claiming that all photography and filming is prohibited. If this happens, you may like to politely point out that the Conditions of Carriage only ban the use of flash and tripods, and if necessary ask the member of staff involved to speak to their supervisor to clarify the position. To be on the safe side, you may wish to approach the on-duty Station Supervisor wherever possible and check that it is OK to take photos. If permission is refused, there may be a good reason for this, such as at busy times or if an event taking place on or near the station which is deemed to require tightened security measures.

▲ Flash photography isn't allowed on the Underground, but today's digital cameras enable good views to be taken without flash. Waterloo & City Line 1992 Stock 65505/506 arrives at Waterloo with a service to Bank on 30 June 2016. **Robert Pritchard**

Map 1

Latimer

to Chalfont &
Latimer
(see Inset A)

Inset A

Watford

Croxley

Moor
Park

Northwood

Northwood
Hills

Pinner

North
Harrow

West Harrow

Harrow-on-
the-Hill

Harrow &
Wealdstone

Kenton

South
Kenton

North
Wembley

Sudbury
Town

Northwick
Park

South
Harrow

Sudbury
Hill

Rayners
Lane

Eastcote

Ruislip
Manor

Ruislip Gardens

South Ruislip

Ruislip

West
Ruislip

Ickenham

Hillingdon

Northolt

Met/Picc

Rickmansworth

Chorleywood

Chalfont &
Latimer

to
Chorleywood

Chesham

Amersham

Stanmore

Canons
Park

Queensbury

Kingsbury

Preston
Road

Wembley
Central

3

Map 2

LONDON UNDERGROUND

Alperton
Hanger Lane
Park Royal
North Ealing
Ealing Broadway
Acton Town
Ea
Con
Gunners
Kew Gardens
Richmond

Perivale

Greenford

Northolt

Uxbridge

South Ealing
Northfields
Boston Manor

Osterley
Hounslow East
Hounslow Central
Hounslow West

Hatton Cross
Heathrow Terminal 4
Heathrow Central Terminals 2 & 3
Heathrow Terminal 5

London Heathrow Airport

KEY

- Station
- Station below surface
- Tunnel

London Underground Lines:

- Bakerloo
- Central
- Circle
- District
- Hammersmith & City
- Jubilee
- Metropolitan
- Northern
- Piccadilly
- Victoria
- Waterloo & City

Map 3

Map 4

Map 5

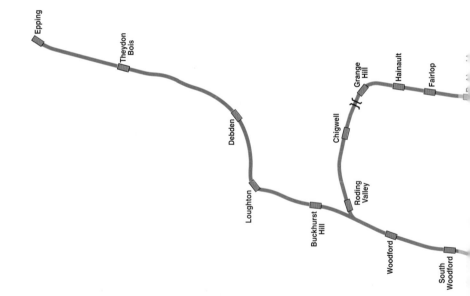

Epping

Theydon Bois

Debden

Loughton

Buckhurst Hill

Chigwell

Grange Hill

Hainault

Fairlop

Roding Valley

Woodford

South Woodford

3

Map 6

1.1. BAKERLOO LINE

Route: Harrow & Wealdstone–Elephant & Castle.
No. of trains: 36 x 7-car (252 cars).   **No. of stations:** 25.

Route length: 14½ miles.
First section opened: 1906.

The Bakerloo Line is one of the shorter London Underground lines, but provides an important link from north-west London to the centre and shopping district of Oxford Street, also linking the main line stations of Paddington, Marylebone (only served by the Bakerloo Line), Charing Cross and Waterloo. The southern terminus at Elephant & Castle is in Zone 1, and (apart from the Waterloo & City line) is the nearest LU terminus to the centre of London.

The Bakerloo Line has its origins in the Baker Street & Waterloo Railway from which it gets its name. Despite this the first section of the line, opened in 1906, actually ran from Baker Street to Elephant & Castle, two stations south of Waterloo, which has been the line's southern terminus since its opening. Construction of the line had started in 1898. The line was extended westwards from Baker Street to Edgware Road via Marylebone in 1907, then on to Paddington in 1913, Queen's Park and Willesden Junction in 1915, and Watford Junction in 1917, running alongside the West Coast Main Line (then owned by the London & North Western Railway) and sharing tracks with the LNWR's Watford DC Line north of Queen's Park.

From 1939 until 1979 the Bakerloo Line also included the Stanmore branch. Since 1979 this has been operated as part of the Jubilee Line (see separate section).

From 1965 Bakerloo Line trains only ran north of Queen's Park in peak hours, since this section was also served by Euston–Watford local trains on the DC Lines. In 1982 Bakerloo Line services were withdrawn north of Stonebridge Park, but were extended back as far as Harrow & Wealdstone in 1984 and restored to run an all day seven days a week service north of Queen's Park in 1989.

The Bakerloo Line south of Queen's Park to Elephant & Castle is all in tunnel, with the northern section from Queen's Park being above ground.

A number of schemes to extend the line have been considered over the years, but have so far never come to fruition. These include a northern extension from Edgware Road to Cricklewood mooted in 1908, and southern extensions to Camberwell proposed in 1931 and 1947. Network Rail's 2011 London & South-East Route Utilisation Strategy envisaged an extension from Elephant & Castle to Lewisham and then on to Hayes via Southeastern's existing line with a possible branch to Beckenham Junction and on to Bromley. A public consultation in 2015 showed strong support for the extension as far as Lewisham, for which Transport for London has now allocated funds in its business plan with completion expected by 2028–29. Any extension beyond Lewisham would be considered as a separate phase at a later date.

SERVICES

The basic all-day service consists of 20 trains per hour on the core section between Elephant & Castle and Queen's Park, giving a train approximately every 3 minutes. Of these, six trains per hour run to and from Harrow & Wealdstone and a further three continue as far as Stonebridge Park. Unlike all other deep level tube lines (apart from the Waterloo & City) there is currently no Night Tube service on the Bakerloo Line. Trains run from around 05.30 to 00.30 on Mondays–Saturdays and from 07.00 to midnight on Sundays.

ROLLING STOCK AND DEPOTS

All Bakerloo Line trains are currently formed of 1972 Tube Stock, which are similar to the (now withdrawn) 1967 Stock used on the Victoria Line until 2011. 63 of these trains were originally built by Metro-Cammell, Birmingham for the Northern Line in two batches; Mark 1 and Mark 2. They were cascaded to the Bakerloo Line from 1977, but were concentrated on the Jubilee Line from 1979. Today 36 trains remain, mainly Mark 2 stock refurbished 1991–95 by Tickford, Rosyth. These trains have been in sole charge on the Bakerloo Line since the mid-1980s following the withdrawal of the earlier 1938 and 1959 Stock, and are expected to remain in service until the introduction of new fully automatic trains by 2033 as part of TfL's New Tube for London programme, by which time the existing fleet will be some 60 years old. Having been refurbished in the mid-1990s, 1972 Stock is currently receiving a life extension at Acton Works, which includes corrosion rectification, new flooring and car body repairs. This work is due for

▲ The Bakerloo Line 1972 Stock is the oldest stock still in normal passenger service with London Underground. 3237/3435 arrives at Kensal Green with an Elephant & Castle service on 11 June 2016. **Robert Pritchard**

▼ 3554/3250 arrive at Marylebone with an Elephant & Castle–Queen's Park service on 11 June 2016. **Robert Pritchard**

completion in 2020. As a separate project cars have also received an interior refurbishment involving the renewal of the lighting, handrails and seat moquette.

The 1972 Stock operates as 7-car fixed formation trains, formed of one south end 4-car and one north end 3-car units, not in permanent formation. The 4-car unit south end DM cab at the centre of the formation is unused in traffic and is generally known as a MM (Middle Motor). 32 of the 36 trains are required for the peak service.

The main depot is at Stonebridge Park; trains also stable at Queen's Park, Elephant & Castle and London Road – near Lambeth North. A unique feature of the depot at Queen's Park is that passenger-carrying trains run through it.

1972 TUBE STOCK   BAKERLOO LINE

Formation: 7-car; DM–T–T–MM (* UNDM) + UNDM–T–DM.
Construction: Aluminium body on steel underframe.
Traction Motors: 4 x DC nose-suspended Brush LT115 of 53 kW (71 hp) per motor car.
Wheel Arrangement: Bo-Bo + 2-2 + 2-2 + Bo-Bo (+) Bo-Bo + 2-2 + Bo-Bo.
Braking: Electro-pneumatic and rheostatic.
Dimensions: 16.09/15.98 x 2.64 m. **Height:** 2.877 m.
Bogies: Plate frame.
Gangways: Emergency end doors only.
Couplers: LU automatic wedgelock.
Control System: Resistor camshaft.
Doors: Sliding.
Maximum Speed: 45 mph.
Train Protection: Tripcock.
Seating Layout: 268 seats, mainly longitudinal but a few 2+2 facing.

DM. Metro-Cammell 1972–74. 40 seats. 27.8 tonnes.
T. Metro-Cammell 1972–74. 36 seats. 18.1 tonnes.
UNDM. Metro-Cammell 1972–74. 40 seats. 26.5 tonnes.
MM. Metro-Cammell 1972–74. 40 seats. 27.8 tonnes.

4-car single-ended units (south end of train)
Cars 4352–4363 are fitted with de-icing equipment.

DM (south)	T	T	MM								
3231	4231	4331	3331	3243	4243	4343	3343	3256	4256	4356	3356
3232	4232	4332	3332	3244	4244	4344	3344	3258	4258	4358	3358
3233	4233	4333	3333	3245	4245	4345	3345	3259	4259	4359	3359
3234	4234	4334	3334	3246	4246	4346	3346	3260	4260	4360	3360
3235	4235	4335	3335	3247	4247	4347	3347	3261	4261	4361	3361
3236	4236	4336	3336	3248	4248	4348	3348	3262	4262	4362	3362
3237	4237	4337	3337	3250	4250	4350	3350	3263	4263	4363	3363
3238	4238	4338	3338	3251	4251	4351	3351	3264	4264	4364	3364
3239	4239	4339	3339	3252	4252	4352	3352	3265	4265	4365	3365
3240	4240	4340	3340	3253	4253	4353	3353	3266	4266	4366	3366
3241	4241	4341	3341	3254	4254	4354	3354	3267	4267	4367	3367
3242	4242	4342	3342	3255	4255	4355	3355	3299	4299	4399	3399*

3-car single-ended units (north end of train)

UNDM	T	DM (north)								
3431	4531	3531	3444	4544	3544	3456	4556	3556
3432	4532	3532	3445	4545	3545	3457	4557	3557
3433	4533	3533	3446	4546	3546	3458	4558	3558
3434	4534	3534	3447	4547	3547	3459	4559	3559
3435	4535	3535	3448	4548	3548	3460	4560	3560
3436	4536	3536	3449	4549	3549	3461	4561	3561
3437	4537	3537	3450	4550	3550	3462	4562	3562
3438	4538	3538	3451	4551	3551	3463	4563	3563
3440	4540	3540	3452	4552	3552	3464	4564	3564
3441	4541	3541	3453	4553	3553	3465	4565	3565
3442	4542	3542	3454	4554	3554	3466	4566	3566
3443	4543	3543	3455	4555	3555	3467	4567	4567

▲ Passing a route map showing the Bakerloo Line's 25 stations, 3267/3446 arrives at the southern terminus at Elephant & Castle on 4 July 2016. **Robert Pritchard**

1.2. PICCADILLY LINE

Route: Uxbridge/Heathrow Airport–Cockfosters.
No. of trains: 86 x 6-car (516 cars).   No. of stations: 53.

Route length: 44 miles.
First section opened: 1869.

The Piccadilly Line links Heathrow – Europe's busiest airport, with central London and King's Cross/St Pancras (notably the only main line terminus served by the line), finishing at Cockfosters in north London.

The Piccadilly has its origins in the Great Northern, Piccadilly & Brompton Railway which was formed in 1902 from a merger of the Brompton & Piccadilly Circus Railway and the Great Northern & Strand Railway. Four years later in 1906, the GNP&BR opened its first section of line between Finsbury Park and Hammersmith.

However, this is not the oldest section of the present-day Piccadilly Line: this honour falls to the Hammersmith–Hounslow West section of the present day Heathrow branch, opened by the District Railway in stages between 1869 and 1884. This section was served only by the DR (later to become the District Line) until 1933 when Piccadilly Line trains began to run as far as Northfields on 9 January and Hounslow West on 13 March. District Line trains ceased serving the Hounslow West branch in 1964, since when it has been operated only by the Piccadilly Line.

Also originally operated by the District Railway was the Acton Town–Rayners Lane branch, opened in 1910. In July 1932 the Piccadilly Line took over this route as far as South Harrow, followed in October 1933 by South Harrow–Rayners Lane–Uxbridge (shared with the Metropolitan Line between Rayners Lane and Uxbridge).

The first new-build extension took the Piccadilly Line from Finsbury Park to its northern terminus at Cockfosters, opened in three stages between September 1932 and July 1933. This would be the last extension of the line for over 40 years until the Hounslow West branch was extended to Hatton Cross in July 1975 (requiring the resiting of Hounslow West station), then on to Heathrow Airport in December 1977.

Since then the expansion of Heathrow Airport has seen the addition of Heathrow Terminal 4 station in April 1986 (when Heathrow Central station was renamed Heathrow Terminals 1, 2, 3; now known as Terminals 2 & 3 following the closure of Terminal 1) and Heathrow Terminal 5 in March 2008. Between 1986 and 2008 all Heathrow trains ran in a clockwise direction around the Heathrow Loop, calling at Terminal 4 station first and then Terminals 1, 2, 3. This pattern still applies to trains serving Terminal 4, but Terminal 5 trains serve Terminals 2 & 3 first before continuing to the Terminal 5 terminus.

The only part of the Piccadilly Line to have closed is the Holborn–Aldwych branch, opened in 1907 and closed in 1994, having operated in peak hours only for many years. This branch was considered for extension to Waterloo on a number of occasions but these plans were never realised. Despite its closure, Aldwych station (originally named Strand) became Grade II listed in 2011. The station and branch have long been a popular filming location.

Also closed (although only ever served by the District Railway) was the Hounslow Town spur, a short triangle branch abandoned in 1909 when the present Hounslow East station (named Hounslow Town until 1925) opened.

Apart from Aldwych, the Piccadilly Line has five other closed stations (all located on operational sections of the line):

• Brompton Road, between South Kensington and Knightsbridge (closed 1934);
• Down Street, between Hyde Park Corner and Green Park (closed 1932, but still booked to be used by occasional empty reversing trains);
• Osterley Park & Spring Grove, between Boston Manor and Osterley (closed 1934 and replaced by the present Osterley station);
• Park Royal & Twyford Abbey, between Alperton and Park Royal (closed 1931 and replaced by the present Park Royal station);
• York Road, between King's Cross St Pancras and Caledonian Road (closed 1932).

A noteworthy feature of the Piccadilly Line is "express" running – between Hammersmith and Acton Town, Piccadilly Line trains don't normally serve four stations that are served by District Line trains.

The Heathrow branch is almost all in tunnel west of Hounslow West. It is then above ground to Barons Court (as is the entire route from Uxbridge). After Barons Court it is in tunnel to

▲ 153/220 arrives at Osterley with a service for Heathrow Terminal 4 on 15 June 2016.
Robert Pritchard

▼ 181/156 arrives at Cockfosters, the northern terminus of the Piccadilly Line, on 5 July 2016.
Robert Pritchard

Arnos Grove, and then above ground to Cockfosters apart from a tunnel around a mile long at Southgate.

SERVICES

The basic off-peak Piccadilly Line service pattern consists of:

* Six trains per hour Cockfosters–Heathrow Terminal 5 (via Terminals 2 & 3);
* Six trains per hour Cockfosters–Heathrow Terminal 4 (returning via Terminals 2 & 3);
* Six trains per hour Cockfosters–Rayners Lane, of which three continue to Uxbridge;
* Three trains per hour Arnos Grove–Northfields.

There are a few early morning short workings between Osterley (starting from Northfields depot) and Heathrow, running alternately to Terminal 4 and Terminal 5, with the first train on Mondays–Fridays leaving Osterley at 04.49. In the other direction the first trains leave Terminal 4 at 05.02 and Boston Manor at 05.18, and the first westbound train along the length of the line leaves Cockfosters at 05.09. The last trains reach Rayners Lane at 00.24, Heathrow Terminal 5 at 00.35, Cockfosters at 00.47 and Arnos Grove at 00.41. There are also a few late night short workings, the last of which starts from Rayners Lane at 00.52 and arrives at Acton Town at 01.16. On Sunday nights the last trains mostly reach their destination between 00.30 and 01.00.

A Night Tube service operates every 10 minutes on Friday and Saturday nights between Heathrow Terminal 5 and Cockfosters.

ROLLING STOCK AND DEPOTS

All services are formed of 1973 Tube Stock, purpose-built for the Piccadilly Line by Metro-Cammell, Birmingham and refurbished 1993–2001 by Bombardier Prorail at Horbury. These trains were a further development of Victoria Line 1967 Tube Stock and 1972 Tube Stock now used on the Bakerloo Line, but modified with longer car bodies and wider vestibules to provide more luggage space for Heathrow Airport passengers. The existing Piccadilly Line fleet is due to be replaced by new fully automatic trains by 2025 as part of the New Tube for London programme.

There are 86 trains formed of two 3-car half units, not in permanent formations. Some are formed of double-ended DM–T–DM units, but two of these are not normally used together in one train. One double-ended unit is formed of three cars from withdrawn half units. 78 trains are required for the peak service.

The main depots are Northfields and Cockfosters. Trains also stable at Uxbridge, South Harrow, and Arnos Grove.

1973 TUBE STOCK   PICCADILLY LINE

Formation: 6-car; DM–T–UNDM + UNDM–T–DM or DM–T–UNDM + DM–T–DM.
Construction: Aluminium body on steel underframe.
Traction Motors: 4 x DC nose-suspended Brush LT118 of 49 kW (65 hp) per motor car.
Wheel Arrangement: Bo-Bo + 2-2 + Bo-Bo (+) Bo-Bo + 2-2 + Bo-Bo.
Braking: Westcode and rheostatic.
Dimensions: 17.47/17.68 x 2.63 m. **Height:** 2.888 m.
Bogies: Plate frame.
Gangways: Emergency end doors only.
Couplers: LU automatic wedgelock.
Control System: Resistor camshaft.
Doors: Sliding.
Maximum Speed: 45 mph.
Train Protection: Tripcock.
Seating Layout: 228 seats, longitudinal.

DM. Metro-Cammell 1974–77. 38 seats. 29.8 tonnes.
T. Metro-Cammell 1974–77. 38 seats. 20.2 tonnes.
UNDM. Metro-Cammell. 1974–77. 38 seats. 28.5 tonnes.

Cars 606–652 (even numbers only) are fitted with de-icing equipment.

▲ 209/184 arrives at leafy Sudbury Hill with an Uxbridge–Cockfosters service on 15 June 2016.

Robert Pritchard

3-car single-ended units

DM	T	UNDM		DM	T	UNDM		DM	T	UNDM
100	500	300		152	552	352		205	605	405
101	501	301		153	553	353		206	606	406
102	502	302		154	554	354		207	607	407
103	503	303		155	555	355		208	608	408
104	504	304		156	556	356		209	609	409
105	505	305		157	557	357		210	610	410
106	506	306		158	558	358		211	611	411
107	507	307		159	559	359		212	612	412
108	508	308		160	560	360		213	613	413
109	509	309		161	561	361		214	614	414
110	510	310		162	562	362		215	615	415
111	511	311		163	563	363		216	616	416
112	512	312		164	564	364		217	617	417
113	513	313		165	565	365		218	618	418
115	515	315		167	567	367		219	619	419
116	516	316		168	568	368		220	620	420
117	517	317		169	569	369		221	621	421
118	518	318		170	570	370		222	622	422
119	519	319		171	571	371		223	623	423
120	520	320		172	572	372		224	624	424
121	521	321		173	573	373		225	625	425
122	522	322		174	574	374		226	626	426
123	523	323		175	575	375		227	627	427
124	524	324		176	576	376		228	628	428
125	525	325		177	577	377		229	629	429
126	526	326		178	578	378		230	630	430
127	527	327		179	579	379		231	631	431
128	528	328		180	580	380		232	632	432
129	529	329		181	581	381		233	633	433
130	530	330		182	582	382		234	634	434
131	531	331		183	583	383		235	635	435
132	532	332		184	584	384		236	636	436
133	533	333		185	585	385		237	637	437
134	534	334		186	586	386		238	638	438
135	535	335		187	587	387		239	639	439
136	536	336		188	588	388		240	640	440
137	537	337		189	589	389		241	641	441
138	538	338		190	590	390		242	642	442
139	539	339		191	591	391		243	643	443
140	540	340		192	592	392		244	644	444
141	541	341		193	593	393		245	645	445
142	542	342		194	594	394		246	646	446
143	543	343		195	595	395		247	647	447
144	544	344		196	596	396		248	648	448
145	545	345		197	597	397		249	649	449
146	546	346		198	598	398		250	650	450
147	547	347		199	599	399		251	651	451
148	548	348		200	600	400		252	652	452
149	549	349		201	601	401		253	653	453
150	550	350		202	602	402				
151	551	351		203	603	403		–	566	366 (S)

3-car double-ended units. * (ex-114 688 889)

DM	T	DM		DM	T	DM		DM	T	DM
854	654	855		868	668	869		882	682	883
856	656	857		870	670	871		884	684	885
858	658	859		872	672	873		886	686	887
860	660	861		874	674	875		890	690	891
862	662	863		876	676	877		892	692	893
864	664	865		878	678	879		894	694	895
866	666	867		880	680	881		896	696	897*

▲ 196/165 arrives at Heathrow Terminals 2 & 3 with a service for Terminal 5 on 15 June 2016.
Robert Pritchard

▼ 863/110 arrives at Rayners Lane on 15 June 2016 with a service for Uxbridge (the Metropolitan Line is seen trailing in from the left). 863 is one of the double-ended units – note the inter-car barrier fixings on the edges of the cab for use when the cab is formed in the middle of a train (rather than the smooth finish). **Robert Pritchard**

1.3. CENTRAL LINE

Route: West Ruislip/Ealing Broadway–Epping/Hainault. **Route length:** 46 miles.
No. of trains: 85 x 8-car (680 cars). **No. of stations:** 49. **First section opened:** 1900.

The Central Line, as its name suggests, runs across the centre of London, from west to east, serving the shopping districts of Oxford Street, the West End and the City of London. The busiest line on the Underground, it starts from the far suburbs of West Ruislip in the west, finishing at Epping in the east: the 34 mile journey between the two stations is the longest possible on LU, taking between 82 and 87 minutes depending on the time of day.

The Central Line was the third deep level Tube line to open, with the initial section between Queen's Road (now Queensway) and King William Street (now Bank) being opened by the Central London Railway Company in 1900. Until 1907, the CLRC charged a 2d flat fare, hence the "Twopenny Tube" nickname. An extension to Wood Lane, near Shepherd's Bush, opened in 1908 to coincide with the Franco-British Exhibition. This was followed by extensions to Liverpool Street in 1912 and Ealing Broadway in 1920.

As part of the London Passenger Transport Board's 1935–40 New Works Programme the line was extended to Greenford in 1947 and West Ruislip in 1948. This programme also saw the Central Line extended eastwards to Stratford and beyond, taking over the existing Great Eastern suburban lines from Leyton to Epping, Ongar, Hainault and Newbury Park in stages between 1946 and 1949 including a new underground section between Leytonstone and Newbury Park to complete the Hainault Loop. The Epping–Ongar section remained steam-operated until 1957 and closed as part of the LU network in 1994, reopening as a heritage operation under the name of the Epping Ongar Railway in 2004.

The western section from White City to Ealing Broadway and West Ruislip is above ground. From White City the line is in tunnel as far as Stratford, where it runs above ground through Stratford station and then goes back into a tunnel as far as the next station, Leyton, from where the rest of the line is above ground except for the tunnel section of the Hainault Loop between Leytonstone and Newbury Park.

SERVICES

The basic off-peak service pattern sees trains running West Ruislip–Epping and Ealing Broadway–Hainault via Newbury Park (some of which continue to Woodford via the top section of the Hainault Loop). These are supplemented by shorter workings such as Ealing Broadway–Newbury Park and Northolt–Loughton. Peak hours see some non-standard workings such as Ealing Broadway–Epping and West Ruislip–Hainault. A total of 24 trains per hour operate on the core central London section, giving a train every 2–3 minutes. This is increased to 26–30 trains per hour in peak periods.

Trains run from around 05.30 to 00.30 on the core section on Mondays–Thursdays, with some short workings between Epping and Loughton until as late as 01.30. The Central Line is one of five Underground lines to operate a Night Tube service on Friday and Saturday nights, with trains running every 20 minutes White City–Hainault via Newbury Park and Ealing Broadway–Loughton, giving a 10-minute service between White City and Leytonstone. On Sunday nights the last trains pass through the central section by around 23.50, reaching the outer ends of the line by around 00.30.

ROLLING STOCK AND DEPOTS

Since its introduction in 1993–95, the 1992 Tube Stock fleet has worked all Central Line services. There are 85 trains formed of four 2-car units in no permanent formation. The 1992 Stock was built by ADtranz (formerly BREL) at Derby. The majority of trains are formed two A+B and two C+B units. A are DM cars with cabs and B and C cabless M cars but with shunting control cabinets. B cars do not have traction pick up shoes. C cars are designated D where fitted with de-icing equipment. All axles on all cars are motored. There are more A than C cars forcing a small number of trains into traffic with boxed-in cabs. All cars received new Siemens bogies from 2011 onwards, replacing the original Kawasaki bogies. 78 trains required for the peak service.

The main Central Line depots are at Hainault and Ruislip; trains also stable at White City, Loughton and Woodford.

▲ Central Line 1992 Stock 91055/92008/92450/91321 passes the attractive lattice footbridge at Theydon Bois with a service for Epping on 19 June 2016. **Robert Pritchard**

▼ 91189/92256/92428/91233 arrives at Grange Hill, on the Hainault loop, with a service for Hainault on 19 June 2016. **Robert Pritchard**

▲ 91225/92184/91253/91249 arrives at the attractive station at Chigwell with a service for Hainault on 19 June 2016. **Robert Pritchard**

1992 TUBE STOCK CENTRAL LINE

Formation: 8-car; DM–M + M–M + M–M + M–DM; some with boxed-in DM formed mid-train.
Construction: Aluminium extrusions.
Traction Motors: 4 x AC fully suspended Brush LT118 of 49 kW (65 hp) per motor car.
Wheel Arrangement: Bo-Bo + Bo-Bo (+) Bo-Bo + Bo-Bo (+) Bo-Bo + Bo-Bo (+) Bo-Bo + Bo-Bo.
Braking: Analogue rheostatic and regenerative.
Dimensions: 16.25 x 2.62 m. **Height:** 2.869 m.
Bogies: Kawasaki H frame (original); rebogied Siemens.
Gangways: Emergency end doors only.
Couplers: LU automatic wedgelock.
Control System: GTO chopper.
Doors: Sliding, externally mounted.
Maximum Speed: 53 mph.
Train Protection: Westinghouse coded track circuit ATC.
Seating Layout: 272 seats, longitudinal.

DM. ADtranz 1991–94. 34 seats. 22.5 tonnes.
M(B). ADtranz 1991–94. 34 seats. 20.5 tonnes.
M(C). ADtranz 1991–94. 34 seats. 21.5 tonnes.

A+B 2-car units

DM	NDM						
91001	92001	91083	92083	91165	92165	91247	92247
91003	92003	91085	92085	91167	92167	91249	92249
91005	92005	91087	92087	91169	92169	91251	92251
91007	92007	91089	92089	91171	92171	91253	92253
91009	92009	91091	92091	91173	92173	91255	92255
91011	92011	91093	92093	91175	92175	91257	92257
91013	92013	91095	92095	91177	92177	91259	92259
91015	92015	91097	92097	91179	92179	91261	92261
91017	92017	91099	92099	91181	92181	91263	92263
91019	92019	91101	92101	91183	92183	91265	92265
91021	92021	91103	92103	91185	92185	91267	92267
91023	92023	91105	92105	91187	92187	91269	92269
91025	92025	91107	92107	91189	92189	91271	92271
91027	92027	91109	92109	91191	92191	91273	92273
91029	92029	91111	92111	91193	92193	91275	92275
91031	92031	91113	92113	91195	92195	91277	92277
91033	92033	91115	92115	91197	92197	91279	92279
91035	92035	91117	92117	91199	92199	91281	92281
91037	92037	91119	92119	91201	92201	91283	92283
91039	92039	91121	92121	91203	92203	91285	92285
91041	92041	91123	92123	91205	92205	91287	92287
91043	92043	91125	92125	91207	92207	91289	92289
91045	92045	91127	92127	91209	92209	91291	92291
91047	92047	91129	92129	91211	92211	91293	92293
91049	92049	91131	92131	91213	92213	91295	92295
91051	92051	91133	92133	91215	92215	91297	92297
91053	92053	91135	92135	91217	92217	91299	92299
91055	92055	91137	92137	91219	92219	91301	92301
91057	92057	91139	92139	91221	92221	91303	92303
91059	92059	91141	92141	91223	92223	91305	92305
91061	92061	91143	92143	91225	92225	91307	92307
91063	92063	91145	92145	91227	92227	91309	92309
91065	92065	91147	92147	91229	92229	91311	92311
91067	92067	91149	92149	91231	92231	91313	92313
91069	92069	91151	92151	91233	92233	91315	92315
91071	92071	91153	92153	91235	92235	91317	92317
91073	92073	91155	92155	91237	92237	91319	92319
91075	92075	91157	92157	91239	92239	91321	92321
91077	92077	91159	92159	91241	92241	91323	92323
91079	92079	91161	92161	91243	92243	91325	92325
91081	92081	91163	92163	91245	92245	91327	92327

▲ 91107/92136/92044/91243 arrive at Holborn with a Loughton service on 19 June 2016.
Robert Pritchard

▼ 91195 leads a West Ruislip service into Tottenham Court Road, one of the busiest stations on the Central Line, on 18 March 2016. **Robert Pritchard**

91329	92329	91335	92335	91341	92341	91347	92347
91331	92331	91337	92337	91343	92343	91349	92349
91333	92333	91339	92339	91345	92345		

B+C 2-car units

NDM	*NDM*						
92002	93002	92070	93070	92136	93136	92202	93202
92004	93004	92072	93072	92138	93138	92204	93204
92006	93006	92074	93074	92140	93140	92206	93206
92008	93008	92076	93076	92142	93142	92208	93208
92010	93010	92078	93078	92144	93144	92210	93210
92012	93012	92080	93080	92146	93146	92212	93212
92014	93014	92082	93082	92148	93148	92214	93214
92016	93016	92084	93084	92150	93150	92216	93216
92018	93018	92086	93086	92152	93152	92218	93218
92020	93020	92088	93088	92154	93154	92220	93220
92022	93022	92090	93090	92156	93156	92222	93222
92024	93024	92092	93092	92158	93158	92224	93224
92026	93026	92094	93094	92160	93160	92226	93226
92028	93028	92096	93096	92162	93162	92228	93228
92030	93030	92098	93098	92164	93164	92230	93230
92032	93032	92100	93100	92166	93166	92232	93232
92034	93034	92102	93102	92168	93168	92234	93234
92036	93036	92104	93104	92170	93170	92236	93236
92038	93038	92106	93106	92172	93172	92238	93238
92040	93040	92108	93108	92174	93174	92240	93240
92042	93042	92110	93110	92176	93176	92242	93242
92044	93044	92112	93112	92178	93178	92244	93244
92046	93046	92114	93114	92180	93180	92246	93246
92048	93048	92116	93116	92182	93182	92248	93248
92050	93050	92118	93118	92184	93184	92250	93250
92052	93052	92120	93120	92186	93186	92252	93252
92054	93054	92122	93122	92188	93188	92254	93254
92056	93056	92124	93124	92190	93190	92256	93256
92058	93058	92126	93126	92192	93192	92258	93258
92060	93060	92128	93128	92194	93194	92260	93260
92062	93062	92130	93130	92196	93196	92262	93262
92064	93064	92132	93132	92198	93198	92264	93264
92066	93066	92134	93134	92200	93200	92266	93266
92068	93068						

B+D 2-car units

NDM	*NDM*						
92402	93402	92418	93418	92434	93434	92450	93450
92404	93404	92420	93420	92436	93436	92452	93452
92406	93406	92422	93422	92438	93438	92454	93454
92408	93408	92424	93424	92440	93440	92456	93456
92410	93410	92426	93426	92442	93442	92458	93458
92412	93412	92428	93428	92444	93444	92460	93460
92414	93414	92430	93430	92446	93446	92462	93462
92416	93416	92432	93432	92448	93448	92464	93464

1.4. WATERLOO & CITY LINE

Route: Waterloo–Bank.
No. of trains: 5 x 4-car (20 cars). **No. of stations:** 2.
Route length: 1½ miles.
First section opened: 1898.

The Waterloo & City Line connects the main line Waterloo station with the city of London at Bank.

The line was opened in 1898 by the Waterloo & City Railway, a subsidiary of the London & South Western Railway created to cater for main line passengers arriving at Waterloo who wished to reach the City of London, which has been the main purpose of the line since its opening. It is unique in being only a shuttle between two stations, with no intermediate stops, and having no physical connection with either the National network or other Underground lines. The northern terminus of the line was originally referred to as City station by the W&CR and as Bank station by the Central London Railway and the City & South London Railway (the original operators of the Central and Northern Lines respectively), the entire station being named Bank since 1940.

Until April 1994, the W&C was operated by British Railways (and its predecessors before railway nationalisation in 1948). With the privatisation of BR, the line became part of London Underground.

SERVICES

Services operate throughout the day from around 06.15–00.30 on Mondays–Fridays. Off-peak trains operate every 5 minutes, and generally every 3 minutes at peak times. Historically the line has only operated on Saturday mornings, but in recent years this has gradually been extended to an almost all-day Saturday service from around 08.00 to 00.30. There is no Sunday or Bank Holiday service.

ROLLING STOCK AND DEPOTS

Only three types of train have operated on the W&C since its opening. From 1898 until 1940 services were worked by EMUs built by the Jackson & Sharp Company of Wilmington, Delaware in the USA. These were then replaced by units built at Dick Kerr Works, Preston, latterly known as Class 487. Finally, in 1993 these distinctive units were replaced by 4-car 1992 Tube Stock (BR Class 482) of the same basic design as those on the Central Line (BR tagged an order for five 4-car units onto the LU order for Central Line 1992 Stock). The units were originally painted in a version of Network SouthEast blue and white livery.

W&C DM and M cars are equivalent to Central Line A and B cars, but are not equipped for Automatic Train Operation, and are designated E and F. Sets are normally paired as consecutively numbered sets (ie 65501+65502). All five trains are required to be in service at peak times, with three required at off-peak times.

The main depot is at Waterloo (just beyond the end of the platforms) and trains also stable at Bank. The isolation of the line from the rest of the LUL and National Rail networks means that trains have to be lifted off the track by cranes whenever they require maintenance work not able to be carried out on site.

1992 TUBE STOCK

WATERLOO & CITY LINE

Formation: 4-car; DM–M + M–DM.
Construction: Aluminium extrusions.
Traction Motors: 4 x AC fully suspended Brush LT118 of 49 kW (65 hp) per motor car.
Wheel Arrangement: Bo-Bo + Bo-Bo (+) Bo-Bo + Bo-Bo.
Braking: Analogue rheostatic and regenerative.
Dimensions: 16.25 x 2.62 m. **Height:** 2.869 m.
Bogies: Kawasaki H frame (original); rebogied Siemens.
Gangways: Emergency end doors only.
Couplers: LU automatic wedgelock.
Control System: GTO chopper.
Doors: Sliding, externally mounted.
Maximum Speed: 53 mph.
Train Protection: Tripcock.
Seating Layout: 136 seats, longitudinal.

DM. ADtranz 1991–94. 34 seats. 22.5 tonnes.
M. ADtranz 1991–94. 34 seats. 21.5 tonnes.

2-car units E (east) + F (middle)

DM	M							
65501	67501	65505	67505	65507	67507	65509	67509
65503	67503							

2-car units F (middle) + E (west)

M	DM							
67502	65502	67506	65506	67508	65508	67510	65510
67504	65504							

▲ Waterloo & City Line 1992 Stock 65503/504 leaves Bank with a service for Waterloo on 30 June 2016. **Robert Pritchard**

1.5. NORTHERN LINE

Route: Edgware/High Barnet/Mill Hill East–Morden via Bank/Charing Cross.
Route length: 36 miles.
No. of trains: 106 x 6-car (636 cars). **No. of stations:** 50. **First section opened:** 1890.

The Northern Line runs from three termini in north London – Edgware, High Barnet and Mill Hill East south to Campden Town where it splits into two routes, one serving Bank and London Bridge and the other Charing Cross and Waterloo. The routes rejoin at Kennington and the line continues to Morden – the most southerly station on LU.

The Northern Line has its origins in the City & South London Railway, London's (and the world's) first deep level tube railway opened between Stockwell and King William Street in 1890. By the turn of the 20th century the C&SL had been extended northwards to Moorgate and southwards to Clapham Common. This was followed by extensions to Angel in 1901 and Euston in 1907.

Also in 1907 the Charing Cross, Euston & Hampstead Railway, having been bought by American financier Charles Yerkes in 1900, opened its own line from Charing Cross to Golders Green with a branch from Camden Town to Archway. In 1913 the Yerkes Group purchased the C&SLR, and further extensions were built between the 1920s and early 1940s. By 1924 the Golders Green branch had reached its present terminus at Edgware, and in 1926 the original CCE&H line was extended southwards to Morden. Finally, the Archway branch was extended to East Finchley in 1939 and High Barnet in 1940, with a short branch being built to Mill Hill East in 1941 (this having been planned to be extended to Edgware).

The name "Northern Line" was first adopted in 1937, ironically after the never realised "Northern Heights" plan to extend the line beyond Edgware to Brockley Hill, Elstree and Bushey Heath. This scheme was included in the 1935–40 New Works Programme, but was abandoned after World War II when the area north of Edgware became part of the Metropolitan Green Belt.

With the formation of the London Passenger Transport Board in 1933, the Great Northern & City Railway between Moorgate and Finsbury Park was made part of what would become the Northern Line. As part of the Northern Heights scheme this line was to have been extended beyond Finsbury Park over the now closed Alexandra Palace branch and via Mill Hill East to Edgware, but these plans never came to fruition, and the Northern City Line remained a self-contained operation until its transfer to British Rail in 1975.

Thus, apart from the disposal of the Northern City Line, the route of the Northern Line has remained unchanged since World War II. Today the Northern Line is the second busiest line on the Underground. A new branch from Kennington to Battersea is planned to be completed by 2020, the first extension for almost 80 years.

Around 70% of the Northern Line is in tunnel. The northern branches of Edgware (to just beyond Golders Green) and High Barnet (to just beyond East Finchley) plus the Mill Hill East branch are above ground, with the rest, apart from the approach to Morden station (and the link line to Morden depot) being in tunnel. The 17-mile tunnel from East Finchley to Morden via Bank is the longest on LU, while 36 of the 50 stations on the Northern Line are underground (the most on any line). It is also worth noting that the line includes both the deepest (Hampstead station with a 55.2 m lift shaft) and the highest point on the LU network above ground level (Dollis Brook Viaduct: 18 m (60 ft)).

SERVICES

For many years all three northern termini (Edgware Road, High Barnet and Mill Hill East) were served by trains from Morden running both via Charing Cross and via Bank. In recent years the service pattern has been simplified so almost all trains via Charing Cross start and finish at Kennington. Only a small number of trains in peak hours and in the early morning and late evening run through to and from Morden via Charing Cross.

The basic off-peak service consists of ten trains per hour on each of the main flows: Edgware–Kennington via Charing Cross, Edgware–Morden via Bank, High Barnet–Kennington via Charing Cross, and High Barnet–Morden via Bank. Trains that terminate at Kennington use the Kennington loop to turn and then return north. This timetable means that from both Edgware and High Barnet trains run alternately to Kennington via Charing Cross and to Morden via Bank, and the entire line has a 20 tph service except for the Mill Hill East branch which operates as a 4 tph shuttle to and from Finchley Central. Mill Hill East, the least used station on the Northern Line, does have a few through trains to Morden and Kennington in the peaks.

▲ Northern Line 1995 Stock 51558/559 arrives at Angel with a service for Morden via Bank on 30 June 2016. There used to just be a narrow island platform here, with tracks either side, but the northbound track has since been moved, hence the wide platforms. **Robert Pritchard**

▼ 51580/579 arrive at Clapham Common, one of two stations on the southern section of the Northern Line that have narrow island platforms, with a service to Edgware via Bank on 4 July 2016. **Robert Pritchard**

Services start at around 05.30 on Mondays–Fridays and finish by 00.30 on Monday–Thursday nights and midnight on Sunday nights. A Night Tube service operates on Friday and Saturday nights, with trains about every 8 minutes between Morden and Camden Town via Charing Cross alternately serving Edgware and High Barnet. Only the Mill Hill East branch and the route via Bank are not served by the Night Tube.

ROLLING STOCK AND DEPOTS

All services are formed of 1995 Tube Stock trains built by GEC Alsthom, Birmingham which first entered service in June 1998 and have worked the Northern Line since the late 1990s, the last Mark 1 1972 Stock trains having been withdrawn in 1999 and the last 1959 Stock in 2000. There are 106 trains (the largest number on any LU line), formed of two 3-car half units in semi-permanent formations. Despite its designation, 1995 Stock was developed after 1996 Stock, with later IGBT traction power electronics replacing the earlier GTO system and other technical differences. Unlike all other LU trains, 1995 Stock is owned by HSBC/RBS (103 trains) or Alstom (three trains) and leased back to LU. 96 trains are required for traffic at peak times, and 80 at off-peak times and at weekends.

The main depots are at Morden and Golders Green. Morden supplies 38 trains into traffic on weekday mornings – the most from any London Underground depot. Trains also stable at Edgware, High Barnet and Highgate.

1995 TUBE STOCK   NORTHERN LINE

Formation: 6-car; DM–T–UNDM + UNDM–T–DM.
Construction: Aluminium extrusions.
Traction Motors: 4 x AC fully suspended GEC G355AZ of 85 kW (114 hp) per motor car.
Wheel Arrangement: Bo-Bo + 2-2 + Bo-Bo (+) Bo-Bo + 2-2 + Bo-Bo.
Braking: Analogue rheostatic and regenerative.
Dimensions: 17.77 x 2.63 m. **Height:** 2.875 m.
Bogies: Flexible box frame.
Gangways: Emergency end doors only.
Couplers: LU automatic wedgelock.
Control System: IGBT.
Doors: Sliding, externally mounted.
Maximum Speed: 45 mph.
Train Protection: Thales Seltrac TBTC.
Seating Layout: 200 seats, longitudinal + 48 tip-ups.

DM. GEC Alsthom 1996–2000. 32 seats + 8 tip-up. 29.4 tonnes.
T. GEC Alsthom 1996–2000. 34 seats + 8 tip-up. 21.5 tonnes.
UNDM. GEC Alsthom 1996–2000. 34 seats + 8 tip-up. 27.9 tonnes.

Cars 52701–726 are fitted with de-icing equipment.

6-car units

DM	T	UNDM	UNDM	T	DM
51501	52501	53501	53701	52701	51701
51502	52502	53502	53503	52503	51503
51504	52504	53504	53505	52505	51505
51506	52506	53506	53507	52507	51507
51508	52508	53508	53702	52702	51702
51509	52509	53509	53510	52510	51510
51511	52511	53511	53512	52512	51512
51513	52513	53513	53514	52514	51514
51515	52515	53515	53703	52703	51703
51516	52516	53516	53517	52517	51517
51518	52518	53518	53519	52519	51519
51520	52520	53520	53704	52704	51704
51521	52521	53521	53522	52522	51522
51523	52523	53523	53524	52524	51524
51525	52525	53525	53705	52705	51705
51526	52526	53526	53527	52527	51527

▲ 51555/554 arrives at Chalk Farm with a service for Edgware on 11 June 2016.

51528	52528	53528	53529	52529	51529
51530	52530	53530	53531	52531	51531
51532	52532	53532	53706	52706	51706
51533	52533	53533	53534	52534	51534
51535	52535	53535	53536	52536	51536
51537	52537	53537	53538	52538	51538
51539	52539	53539	53707	52707	51707
51540	52540	53540	53541	52541	51541
51542	52542	53542	53543	52543	51543
51544	52544	53544	53545	52545	51545
51546	52546	53546	53708	52708	51708
51547	52547	53547	53548	52548	51548
51549	52549	53549	53550	52550	51550
51551	52551	53551	53711	52711	51711
51553	52553	53553	53709	52709	51709
51554	52554	53554	53555	52555	51555
51556	52556	53556	53557	52557	51557
51558	52558	53558	53559	52559	51559
51560	52560	53560	53710	52710	51710
51561	52561	53561	53562	52562	51562
51563	52563	53563	53564	52564	51564
51565	52565	53565	53566	52566	51566
51567	52567	53567	53552	52552	51552
51568	52568	53568	53569	52569	51569
51570	52570	53570	53571	52571	51571
51572	52572	53572	53573	52573	51573
51574	52574	53574	53712	52712	51712
51575	52575	53575	53576	52576	51576
51577	52577	53577	53578	52578	51578
51579	52579	53579	53580	52580	51580

▲ 51685/686 leaves Edgware with a service for Morden via Bank on 11 June 2016. **Robert Pritchard**

51581	52581	53581	53713	52713	51713
51582	52582	53582	53583	52583	51583
51584	52584	53584	53585	52585	51585
51586	52586	53586	53587	52587	51587
51588	52588	53588	53714	52714	51714
51589	52589	53589	53590	52590	51590
51591	52591	53591	53592	52592	51592
51593	52593	53593	53594	52594	51594
51595	52595	53595	53715	52715	51715
51596	52596	53596	53597	52597	51597
51598	52598	53598	53599	52599	51599
51600	52600	53600	53601	52601	51601
51602	52602	53602	53716	52716	51716
51603	52603	53603	53604	52604	51604
51605	52605	53605	53606	52606	51606
51607	52607	53607	53608	52608	51608
51609	52609	53609	53717	52717	51717
51610	52610	53610	53611	52611	51611
51612	52612	53612	53613	52613	51613
51614	52614	53614	53615	52615	51615
51616	52616	53616	53718	52718	51718
51617	52617	53617	53618	52618	51618
51619	52619	53619	53620	52620	51620
51621	52621	53621	53622	52622	51622
51623	52623	53623	53719	52719	51719
51624	52624	53624	53625	52625	51625
51626	52626	53626	53627	52627	51627
51628	52628	53628	53629	52629	51629
51630	52630	53630	53720	52720	51720
51631	52631	53631	53632	52632	51632
51633	52633	53633	53634	52634	51634
51635	52635	53635	53636	52636	51636
51637	52637	53637	53721	52721	51721
51638	52638	53638	53639	52639	51639
51640	52640	53640	53641	52641	51641
51642	52642	53642	53643	52643	51643
51644	52644	53644	53722	52722	51722
51645	52645	53645	53646	52646	51646
51647	52647	53647	53648	52648	51648
51649	52649	53649	53650	52650	51650
51651	52651	53651	53723	52723	51723
51652	52652	53652	53653	52653	51653
51654	52654	53654	53655	52655	51655
51656	52656	53656	53657	52657	51657
51658	52658	53658	53724	52724	51724
51659	52659	53659	53660	52660	51660
51661	52661	53661	53662	52662	51662
51663	52663	53663	53664	52664	51664
51665	52665	53665	53725	52725	51725
51666	52666	53666	53667	52667	51667
51668	52668	53668	53669	52669	51669
51670	52670	53670	53671	52671	51671
51672	52672	53672	53726	52726	51726
51673	52673	53673	53674	52674	51674
51675	52675	53675	53676	52676	51676
51677	52677	53677	53678	52678	51678
51679	52679	53679	53680	52680	51680
51681	52681	53681	53682	52682	51682
51683	52683	53683	53684	52684	51684
51685	52685	53685	53686	52686	51686

▲ 51627/626 arrive at Tooting Bec with a service for Edgware via Bank on 4 July 2016.
Robert Pritchard

▼ 51630/720 arrives at Woodside Park, passing the long-closed signal box, with a High Barnet–Kennington via Charing Cross train on 12 June 2016. **Robert Pritchard**

1.6. JUBILEE LINE

Route: Stanmore–Stratford.
No. of trains: 63 x 7-car (441 cars).   **No. of stations:** 27.
Route length: 22½ miles.
First section opened: 1932.

The Jubilee Line, the newest of the deep Tube lines, runs from Stanmore in north London through to Waterloo before heading east to Canary Wharf and Stratford.

The northern section of the Jubilee Line, between Baker Street and Stanmore, is the oldest stretch of the line and has its origins in the Metropolitan Railway's branch from Wembley Park to Stanmore, opened in 1932. For the first seven years of its life, this line simply operated as a branch of the Metropolitan. From 1939 Baker Street–Stanmore became a branch of the Bakerloo Line from Elephant & Castle, with this arrangement continuing until the opening of the new section between Baker Street and Charing Cross via Bond Street in 1979 when the "Jubilee Line" name came into being and took over the Stanmore branch.

When the extension south from Baker Street was being planned in the 1970s, it was envisaged that the line would later be extended beyond Charing Cross into South-East London and the Docklands, following a route beneath Fleet Street. Because of this, it was to be named the Fleet Line. In the event, this scheme as it was then proposed never came to fruition, and in 1977 the name Jubilee Line was chosen instead to mark Queen Elizabeth II's Silver Jubilee that year.

In the 1980s and 1990s the regeneration of London's Docklands led to a revival of plans to extend the line eastwards. These eventually resulted in the Jubilee Line Extension scheme which took the line to a new terminus at Stratford. Opening in 1999, the new section left the existing line between Green Park and its Charing Cross terminus, serving Westminster, Waterloo, London Bridge and Canary Wharf. An interchange with the East London Railway was built at Canada Water, and a new station and bus interchange was also provided at North Greenwich to serve the Millennium Dome (now the O2 Arena). The eastern extension opened in three stages starting with Stratford–North Greenwich in May 1999. Completion of this extension in November 1999 led to the closure of the line's previous terminus at Charing Cross to regular services, but it is still occasionally used for diversions during disruption and for filming.

Platform edge doors, which line up with the train doors, are fitted at all tunnel stations on the eastern extension from Westminster to North Greenwich. These are a novel feature on the London Underground but have been used on the metros in Singapore and Lille, France since the 1980s. They are also being used on the new "Elizabeth Line" (Crossrail) route through London.

The Stanmore–Finchley Road and Canning Town–Stratford sections are above ground, and Finchley Road–Canning Town is in tunnel.

SERVICES

The basic off-peak service consists of 23–24 trains per hour on the core section between Willesden Green and North Greenwich, giving a 2–3 minute service frequency. Of these, between 12 and 15 trains cover the entire line between Stanmore and Stratford. The rest are short workings covering the centre section of the Line, such as Willesden Green–Stratford, Wembley Park–North Greenwich or Stanmore–West Ham. The peak service sees 30 trains per hour in both directions on the middle section of the Line.

Trains start running at around 05.30 on Mondays–Fridays, finishing between 00.45 and 01.00 on Monday–Thursday nights and around midnight on Sunday nights. A Night Tube service operates every 10 minutes along the entire line on Friday and Saturday nights.

ROLLING STOCK AND DEPOTS

Since 1998 the Jubilee Line has been operated by trains of 1996 Stock, built by GEC Alsthom-Metro-Cammell (now Alstom), Birmingham to replace the short-lived 1983 Stock. There are 63 7-car trains formed of one north end 3-car plus one south end 4-car unit. The 1996 Stock is of a similar design to the 1995 Stock used on the Northern Line. Despite its designation the 1996 Stock was actually developed before 1995 Stock, 1996 Stock having older GTO traction systems and other detail differences.

Originally 59 6-car trains were built, all augmented to 7-cars in 2005. At the same time four completely new 7-car trains were built. The additional units and seventh cars were built by CAF,

▲ Shortly after emerging into daylight, 96046/073 runs alongside the Metropolitan Line and Chiltern main line from Marylebone (to the right) as it arrives at West Hampstead with a service for Stanmore on 5 July 2016. A train of S8 Stock can be seen approaching in the background.

Robert Pritchard

▼ 96066/067 arrives at Baker Street with a Stanmore service on 19 June 2016. **Robert Pritchard**

Zaragoza, Spain for Alstom, retaining the original design traction packs. 58 trains are required for the peak service.

The main depot is at Stratford Market, between Stratford and West Ham stations. The was constructed as part of the Stratford extension – before that Jubilee Line trains had been based at Neasden. Today trains also still stable at Neasden depot (which is shared with the Metropolitan Line) and at Stanmore.

1996 TUBE STOCK   JUBILEE LINE

Formation: 7-car; DM–T–T–UNDM + UNDM–T–DM.
Construction: Aluminium extrusions.
Traction Motors: 4 x AC fully suspended GEC LT200 of 90 kW (120 hp) per motor car.
Wheel Arrangement: Bo-Bo + 2-2 + Bo-Bo (+) Bo-Bo + 2-2 + 2-2 + Bo-Bo.
Braking: Analogue rheostatic and regenerative.
Dimensions: 17.77 x 2.63 m. **Height:** 2.875 m.
Bogies: Flexible box frame.
Gangways: Emergency end doors only.
Couplers: LU automatic wedgelock.
Control System: GTO.
Doors: Sliding, externally mounted.
Maximum Speed: 62 mph.
Train Protection: Thales Seltrac TBTC.
Seating Layout: 238 seats, longitudinal.

DM. GEC Alsthom 1996–98 or * CAF Zaragoza, Spain 2005. 32 seats. 30.0 tonnes.
T. GEC Alsthom 1996–98 or * CAF Zaragoza, Spain 2005. 34 seats. 20.9 tonnes.
UNDM. GEC Alsthom 1996–98 or * CAF Zaragoza, Spain 2005. 34 seats. 27.1 tonnes.

4-car single-ended units

DM (east)	T	T*	UNDM				
96001	96201	96601*	96401	96065	96265	96665*	96465
96003	96203	96603*	96403	96067	96267	96667*	96467
96005	96205	96605*	96405	96069	96269	96669*	96469
96007	96207	96607*	96407	96071	96271	96671*	96471
96009	96209	96609*	96409	96073	96273	96673*	96473
96011	96211	96611*	96411	96075	96275	96675*	96475
96013	96213	96613*	96413	96077	96277	96677*	96477
96015	96215	96615*	96415	96079	96279	96679*	96479
96017	96217	96617*	96417	96081	96281	96681*	96481
96019	96219	96619*	96419	96083	96283	96683*	96483
96021	96221	96621*	96421	96085	96285	96685*	96485
96023	96223	96623*	96423	96087	96287	96687*	96487
96025	96225	96625*	96425	96089	96289	96689*	96489
96027	96227	96627*	96427	96091	96291	96691*	96491
96029	96229	96629*	96429	96093	96293	96693*	96493
96031	96231	96631*	96431	96095	96295	96695*	96495
96033	96233	96633*	96433	96097	96297	96697*	96497
96035	96235	96635*	96435	96099	96299	96699*	96499
96037	96237	96637*	96437	96101	96301	96701*	96501
96039	96239	96639*	96439	96103	96303	96703*	96503
96041	96241	96641*	96441	96105	96305	96705*	96505
96043	96243	96643*	96443	96107	96307	96707*	96507
96045	96245	96645*	96445	96109	96309	96709*	96509
96047	96247	96647*	96447	96111	96311	96711*	96511
96049	96249	96649*	96449	96113	96313	96713*	96513
96051	96251	96651*	96451	96115	96315	96715*	96515
96053	96253	96653*	96453	96117	96317	96717*	96517
96055	96255	96655*	96455	96119*	96319*	96719*	96519*
96057	96257	96657*	96457	96121*	96321*	96721*	96521*
96059	96259	96659*	96459	96123*	96323*	96723*	96523*
96061	96261	96661*	96461	96125*	96325*	96725*	96525*
96063	96263	96663*	96463				

3-car single-ended units

Cars 96880–918 are fitted with de-icing equipment.

UNDM	T	DM (west)
96402	96202	96002
96404	96204	96004
96406	96206	96006
96408	96208	96008
96410	96210	96010
96412	96212	96012
96414	96214	96014
96416	96216	96016
96418	96218	96018
96420	96220	96020
96422	96222	96022
96424	96224	96024
96426	96226	96026
96428	96228	96028
96430	96230	96030
96432	96232	96032
96434	96234	96034
96436	96236	96036
96438	96238	96038
96440	96240	96040
96442	96242	96042

96444	96244	96044
96446	96246	96046
96448	96248	96048
96450	96250	96050
96452	96252	96052
96454	96254	96054
96456	96256	96056
96458	96258	96058
96460	96260	96060
96462	96262	96062
96464	96264	96064
96466	96266	96066
96468	96268	96068
96470	96270	96070
96472	96272	96072
96474	96274	96074
96476	96276	96076
96478	96278	96078
96480	96880	96080
96482	96882	96082
96484	96884	96084

96486	96886	96086
96488	96888	96088
96490	96890	96090
96492	96892	96092
96494	96894	96094
96496	96896	96096
96498	96898	96098
96500	96900	96100
96502	96902	96102
96504	96904	96104
96506	96906	96106
96508	96908	96108
96510	96910	96110
96512	96912	96112
96514	96914	96114
96516	96916	96116
96518	96918	96118
96520*	96320*	96120*
96522*	96322*	96122*
96524*	96324*	96124*
96526*	96326*	96126*

▲ The Jubilee Line 1996 Stock looks very similar to the Northern Line 1995 Stock, but has a very different traction package. 96069/102 arrives at Green Park with a service for North Greenwich on 19 June 2016. **Robert Pritchard**

▲ 96103/100 arrives at Canons Park with a Stanmore–Stratford service on 11 June 2016.
Robert Pritchard

▼ 96114/099 (left) and 96034/093 (right) pass at Neasden on 5 July 2016. Jubilee Line trains serve the Neasden stop, with Metropolitan Line trains running through non-stop.   **Robert Pritchard**

1.7. VICTORIA LINE

Route: Walthamstow Central–Brixton.
No. of trains: 47 x 8-car (376 cars). **No. of stations:** 16.
Route Length: 13½ miles.
First section opened: 1968.

The Victoria Line, running from Walthamstow Central in north-west London to Brixton in south London, is unique in at least three ways: it is the only line to have been built completely from scratch since World War II, the only line to have used Automatic Train Operation since its opening, and the only line (apart from the Waterloo & City) to run entirely in tunnels with no above-ground sections used by passenger-carrying trains. It was originally conceived as an express Tube line from Victoria to Finsbury Park in the late 1930s which would then have taken over a number of LNER lines from Liverpool Street.

After World War II this scheme evolved into a Victoria–Walthamstow line which would eventually materialise with the opening of the Walthamstow Central–Highbury & Islington section in September 1968, continuing to Warren Street in December of that year and finally to Victoria in March 1969.

In the immediate post-war period London County Council's County of London Plan had envisaged a southern extension of the Victoria Line from Victoria to Brixton, Streatham, Norbury and East Croydon. In the event only the Victoria–Brixton section saw the light of day, opening in July 1971 with an intermediate station at Vauxhall. A second station at Pimlico followed in September 1972, the only station on the line not to have interchange with another Underground line or with National Rail or London Overground services.

▲ 11013/014 arrives at Warren Street with southbound service for Brixton on 12 June 2016.
Robert Pritchard

SERVICES

Most trains cover the entire line, but there are a few short workings that start or terminate at Seven Sisters particularly in the early morning and late evening when trains start and finish their day's work at Seven Sisters depot. There is also one early morning train that starts at Victoria, but otherwise all trains start or terminate at Brixton. The basic off-peak service pattern sees a train every 2–3 minutes. This is increased to less than every 2 minutes during peak hours, amounting to 33 trains per hour and giving the most intensive train service on any railway in the UK. The Victoria Line is the most intensively used line in terms of the average number of journeys per mile.

The Victoria Line is one of five Underground lines to operate a Night Tube service on Friday and Saturday nights, with trains running every 10 minutes on the entire line. Otherwise, trains run from around 05.30–00.10 Mondays–Thursdays, finishing at around midnight on Sunday nights.

ROLLING STOCK AND DEPOTS

All services are formed of 2009 Tube Stock, which entered service between 2009 and 2011 replacing the 1967 Stock which had been used since the line opened. The 2009 Stock trains are 3 m longer than their predecessors, making them the second longest trains operated by London Underground (at 133.28 m over couplers) after the S8 Stock (133.47 m). There are 47 8-car trains built by Bombardier, Derby which operate in permanent formations. Early pre-production cars forming complete test trains were built for development only; they were never delivered to LU and are believed to have since been broken up. 39 trains are required for the peak service.

The main depot is at Northumberland Park, which is reached via a branch diverging from the Victoria line to the north of Seven Sisters station. The depot is the only part of the line that is above ground, and is located adjacent to Northumberland Park station on the London Liverpool Street–Cambridge main line. Trains also stable at Walthamstow Central, Victoria and Brixton.

2009 TUBE STOCK   VICTORIA LINE

Formation: 8-car; DM–T–NDM–UNDM + UNDM–NDM–T–DM.
Construction: Bolted and welded aluminium extrusions.
Traction Motors: 4 x AC fully suspended Bombardier Mitrac of 75 kW (100 hp) per motor car.
Wheel Arrangement: Bo-Bo + 2-2 + Bo-Bo + Bo-Bo (+) Bo-Bo + Bo-Bo + 2-2 + Bo-Bo.
Braking: Analogue rheostatic and regenerative.
Dimensions: 16.60/16.35 x 2.616 m. **Height:** 2.883 m.
Bogies: Flexible frame (Bombardier).
Gangways: Emergency end doors only.
Couplers: LU automatic wedgelock with pneumatic connections.
Control System: IGBT.
Doors: Sliding, externally mounted.
Maximum Speed: 50 mph.
Train Protection: Westinghouse DTGR.
Seating Layout: 252 seats, longitudinal + 36 tip-ups.

DM. Bombardier 2009–11. 32 seats + 4 tip-ups. 27.1 tonnes.
T. Bombardier 2009–11. 32 seats + 4 tip-ups. 21.6 tonnes.
NDM. Bombardier 2009–11. 32 seats + 4 tip-ups. 23.8 tonnes.
UNDM. Bombardier 2009–11. 30 + 6 tip-ups. 25.8 tonnes.

8-car units

DM (south)	T	NDM	UNDM	UNDM	NDM	T	DM (north)
11001	12001	13001	14001	14002	13002	12002	11002
11003	12003	13003	14003	14004	13004	12004	11004
11005	12005	13005	14005	14006	13006	12006	11006
11007	12007	13007	14007	14008	13008	12008	11008
11009	12009	13009	14009	14010	13010	12010	11010
11011	12011	13011	14011	14012	13012	12012	11012
11013	12013	13013	14013	14014	13014	12014	11014
11015	12015	13015	14015	14016	13016	12016	11016
11017	12017	13017	14017	14018	13018	12018	11018
11019	12019	13019	14019	14020	13020	12020	11020

▲ Victoria Line 2009 Stock 11005/006 arrives at Brixton, the southern terminus of the line, with a service from Walthamstow Central on 18 June 2016. *Peter Pritchard*

1021	12021	13021	14021	14022	13022	12022	11022
1023	12023	13023	14023	14024	13024	12024	11024
1025	12025	13025	14025	14026	13026	12026	11026
1027	12027	13027	14027	14028	13028	12028	11028
1029	12029	13029	14029	14030	13030	12030	11030
1031	12031	13031	14031	14032	13032	12032	11032
1033	12033	13033	14033	14034	13034	12034	11034
1035	12035	13035	14035	14036	13036	12036	11036
1037	12037	13037	14037	14038	13038	12038	11038
1039	12039	13039	14039	14040	13040	12040	11040
1041	12041	13041	14041	14042	13042	12042	11042
1043	12043	13043	14043	14044	13044	12044	11044
1045	12045	13045	14045	14046	13046	12046	11046
1047	12047	13047	14047	14048	13048	12048	11048
1049	12049	13049	14049	14050	13050	12050	11050
1051	12051	13051	14051	14052	13052	12052	11052
1053	12053	13053	14053	14054	13054	12054	11054
1055	12055	13055	14055	14056	13056	12056	11056
1057	12057	13057	14057	14058	13058	12058	11058
1059	12059	13059	14059	14060	13060	12060	11060
1061	12061	13061	14061	14062	13062	12062	11062
1063	12063	13063	14063	14064	13064	12064	11064
1065	12065	13065	14065	14066	13066	12066	11066
1067	12067	13067	14067	14068	13068	12068	11068
1069	12069	13069	14069	14070	13070	12070	11070
1071	12071	13071	14071	14072	13072	12072	11072
1073	12073	13073	14073	14074	13074	12074	11074
1075	12075	13075	14075	14076	13076	12076	11076
1077	12077	13077	14077	14078	13078	12078	11078
1079	12079	13079	14079	14080	13080	12080	11080
1081	12081	13081	14081	14082	13082	12082	11082
1083	12083	13083	14083	14084	13084	12084	11084
1085	12085	13085	14085	14086	13086	12086	11086
1087	12087	13087	14087	14088	13088	12088	11088
1089	12089	13089	14089	14090	13090	12090	11090
1091	12091	13091	14091	14092	13092	12092	11092
1093	12093	13093	14093	14094	13094	12094	11094

▲ Vauxhall offers interchange with the South West Trains station. On 18 June 2016 11021/022 arrives with a service for Brixton.
Robert Pritchard

1.8. SUB-SURFACE LINES

The four Sub-Surface Lines together make up almost 40% of the London Underground network. 192 new S Stock trains built by Bombardier, Derby have revolutionised the Sub-Surface Lines over the last seven years, replacing all of the ageing A60, C and D78 Stock trains and creating a uniform fleet across all SSLs for the first time in the history of the London Underground (the only difference being that the S7 Stock is formed of 7-car trains with all longitudinal seating while the S8 Stock is made up of 8-cars with some facing bays of seats). This order for 1404 vehicles is the largest ever single rolling stock order placed for the same design of UK rolling stock. They are the first London Underground trains to be fitted with air conditioning.

1.8.1. CIRCLE LINE

Route: Hammersmith/Edgware Road–Liverpool Street–Victoria–Edgware Road (circle).
Route Length: 17 miles.
No. of trains: 132 x 7-car (938 cars)*. **No. of stations:** 36. **First section opened:** 1863.
* Fleet shared with the District and Hammersmith & City Lines.

The Circle Line no longer operates as a true "circle", but more a "teacup" arrangement. As described below, trains run from Hammersmith to Edgware Road, then in a clockwise circle around the centre of London before reaching Edgware Road again: they then return to Hammersmith in an anti-clockwise direction.

The line has its origins in the Metropolitan Railway's original Underground line between Paddington and Farringdon, opened in 1863 (see Metropolitan and Hammersmith & City lines). In the same year a parliamentary select committee report recommended an "inner circle" connecting the existing MR line with London's main line rail termini at Blackfriars, Cannon Street, Charing Cross and Victoria. 1864 saw the formation of the Metropolitan District Railway to open a line from South Kensington to Tower Hill (see District Line).

After being built in stages, enough of the line had been completed to allow the introduction of an Inner Circle service between Moorgate and Mansion House via High Street Kensington on 3 July 1871. 11 years later, in 1882, the Tower Hill–Aldgate section opened, followed by Mansion House–Tower Hill in 1884 when a circular service around the entire circle started initially steam-hauled until electrification was completed in 1905.

The Circle Line appeared as a unique line on the LU maps from 1949, coloured yellow. The line is unique in that its entire route (apart from the very short sections between Aldgate and Tower Hill and the curve between High Street Kensington and Gloucester Road) is shared with other lines: the Hammersmith & City Line between Hammersmith and Edgware Road and on the top part of the circle as far as Liverpool Street (plus the Metropolitan Line between Baker Street and Aldgate), and the District Line between Gloucester Road and Tower Hill. There are no stations served only by the Circle Line.

Whereas the Hammersmith branch is almost all above ground (see Hammersmith & City Line) the entire route of the original Circle Line is in tunnel apart from a few short gaps in the tunnels including those at Notting Hill Gate, Paddington (District/Circle Line platforms), Edgware Road, Farringdon and Barbican stations.

SERVICES

From 1884 until December 2009, the Circle Line operated as a continuous circle without a fixed terminus. This was then changed so that Circle Line trains start from Hammersmith, following the route of the Hammersmith & City Line, then joining the existing Circle Line at Edgware Road where they terminate after doing a complete circuit. They then return round the circle in an anticlockwise direction before terminating back at Hammersmith. This pattern of operation was introduced to make it easier to recover the service more quickly in case of disruption on any part of the route, but means that passengers making journeys such as Gloucester Road–Baker Street or Notting Hill Gate–Euston Square now always have to change at Edgware Road. Service frequencies between Hammersmith and Edgware Road were also almost doubled as a result of this change.

The basic off-peak Circle Line service pattern sees six trains per hour in each direction, approximately every 10 minutes, but these are complemented by District, Metropolitan and Hammersmith & City Line trains along almost the entire route. Services run from around 05.30–00.30 Mondays–Saturdays and 07.00–midnight on Sundays.

Some early morning trains start from Barking and run as far as Tower Hill following the route of the District Line, then continue to Edgware Road as Circle Line trains. In the other direction there are two late night trains (one on Sundays) that start from Aldgate, run a full clockwise circuit of the Circle Line to Liverpool Street and then continue to Barking.

1.8.2. DISTRICT LINE

Route: Ealing Broadway/Richmond/Wimbledon/Kensington Olympia–Edgware Road/Upminster.
Route Length: 40 miles.
No. of trains: 132 x 7-car (938 cars)*.   **No. of stations:** 60.   **First section opened:** 1868.
* Fleet shared with the Circle and Hammersmith & City Lines.

The District Line is a complex operation, running from termini in west and south-west London (Ealing Broadway, Richmond and Wimbledon) to Edgware Road or across the south of London to Barking or Upminster, the easternmost station on LU. The District Line has 60 stations, the highest of any LU line, although more than half of them are shared with other lines.

Only a year after the formation of the Metropolitan Railway, 1864 saw the establishment of the Metropolitan District Railway (soon shortened to the District Railway to avoid confusion) to which the present-day District Line can trace its origins. The first section of what is now the District Line opened between Paddington, Gloucester Road and Westminster in 1868 (although High Street Kensington–Gloucester Road is used only by the Circle Line), and the line was then extended in stages, reaching Tower Hill in 1882. The last few decades of the 19th century also saw extensions to Ealing Broadway, Kensington Olympia, Hounslow, Richmond and Wimbledon, followed by Upminster in 1902, Rayners Lane via Park Royal in 1910, and in 1926 the Wimbledon–High Street Kensington service was extended to Edgware Road (although this section had already been open as part of the Inner Circle since 1871 – see Circle Line).

For many years the Hounslow West branch (since extended to Heathrow Airport) was served both by District and Piccadilly Line trains, until the District Line ceased to operate to Hounslow in 1964. The Acton Town–Rayners Lane via Park Royal line was served by the District Railway for its first 23 years of existence before being taken over by the Piccadilly Line in 1933.

The only part of the District Line now closed, and not served by any other lines, is the Acton Town–South Acton shuttle, opened in 1905 as a through service between South Acton and Hounslow Barracks, reduced to a self-contained shuttle service in 1932 and withdrawn in 1959. Another unusual service operated by the District Line in the early part of the 20th century was the seasonal Ealing–Southend excursion trains which ran from 1910 to 1939. These were hauled by electric locos as far as Barking and then by steam.

The easternmost section between Bow Road and Upminster is above ground, as are the three western branches between Gloucester Road and Ealing Broadway, Richmond and Wimbledon. The central section between Gloucester Road and Bow Road, and the Edgware Road branch between Earl's Court and Edgware Road, are in tunnel, but there are gaps in the tunnels at South Kensington, High Street Kensington, Notting Hill Gate, Edgware Road and Whitechapel stations.

SERVICES

Service patterns have altered little since the withdrawal of District Line services from the Hounslow branch. The District Line can be said to be broadly divided into two distinct parts: the District Main Line via Victoria, served by trains running between Ealing Broadway, Richmond or Wimbledon in the west and Barking, Dagenham East or Upminster in the east (with some trains starting and terminating at Tower Hill), and the Wimbledon–Edgware Road section. Wimbledon is the only one of the three western termini to be served by both Edgware Road and Main Line trains. The High Street Kensington–Olympia shuttle currently operates only at weekends and Bank Holidays, and on weekdays during major events at the Olympia exhibition centre (a limited early morning and evening service operates to and from Olympia on weekdays at other times).

The hub of the District Line can be said to be Earl's Court. On Mondays–Saturdays the first trains begin their journeys at around 04.50 and the last trains reach their destinations between 00.45 and 01.40. Sunday services run from around 06.00 to midnight. The basic off peak service consists of:

- Six trains per hour Ealing Broadway–Upminster;
- Six trains per hour Richmond–Upminster;
- Six trains per hour Wimbledon–Edgware Road;
- Six trains per hour Wimbledon–Tower Hill (three of which continue to Barking);
- Three trains per hour High Street Kensington–Olympia at weekends only.

1.8.3. HAMMERSMITH & CITY LINE

Route: Hammersmith–Barking.
No. of trains: 132 x 7-car (938 cars)*. **No. of stations:** 29.
* Fleet shared with the Circle and District Lines.

Route Length: 16 miles.
First section opened: 1863.

The Hammersmith & City Line runs from Hammersmith in west London via Paddington and the top part of the Circle Line to Liverpool Street, and then along the District Line tracks to Barking.

The western section of the Hammersmith & City Line, between Paddington and Hammersmith, was opened in 1864 by the Hammersmith & City Railway, a subsidiary of the Great Western Railway. It is thus the second oldest section of the London Underground, having opened only a year after the Metropolitan Railway's initial stretch from Paddington to Farringdon Street, which does now also form part of the Hammersmith & City Lines route. For its first year of operation, the Hammersmith branch ran as a broad gauge line with through services to Farringdon Street on the MR. In 1865 the Hammersmith branch became standard (4 ft 8½ in/1435 mm) gauge and a broad gauge service between Paddington and Addison Road (now Kensington Olympia) started. The Addison Road service used a spur onto the West London Line from Latimer Road, closed in 1940.

The short section from Liverpool Street to Aldgate East is the only section of the line used exclusively by H&C trains. Apart from this, Edgware Road–Hammersmith was also not used by any other lines until the extension of Circle Line services to Hammersmith in 2009. All other sections served by the H&C have always been shared with other lines: Edgware Road–Liverpool Street is also used by the Circle Line (plus the Metropolitan Line east of Baker Street) and Aldgate East–Barking is shared with the District Line.

The Hammersmith & City Line formed part of the Metropolitan Line until 1990 when it received its own separate identity and pink colour on the LU maps.

All of the Hammersmith branch is above ground apart from the Subway Tunnel, which takes the line under the Great Western Main Line between Royal Oak and Westbourne Park. At the west end much of the route is elevated on viaducts, giving good views of the west London cityscape.

SERVICES

Historically, H&C trains have only continued beyond Whitechapel in peak hours, but today almost all trains run along the entire length of the line between Hammersmith and Barking.

The basic off-peak service pattern sees six trains per hour between Hammersmith and Barking, running at intervals of between 9 and 11 minutes. Combined with the Circle Line this gives 12 trains per hour between Hammersmith and Liverpool Street via Edgware Road and Baker Street. On Mondays–Saturdays the first trains leave Hammersmith as early as 04.38 and Barking at 05.01, and the last trains terminate at Hammersmith at 01.07 and Barking at 01.18. On Sundays the first trains leave Barking at 06.26 and Hammersmith at 06.31 (preceded by the first Circle Line train from Hammersmith at 06.21) and the last trains leave Barking at 23.53 and Hammersmith at 23.46.

1.8.4. METROPOLITAN LINE

Route: Uxbridge/Amersham/Chesham/Watford–Aldgate. **Route Length:** 41½ miles.
No. of trains: 60 x 8-car (464 cars). **No. of stations:** 34. **First section opened:** 1863.

The Metropolitan Line operates longer distance services from the far suburbs of Amersham, Chesham and Watford, and also Uxbridge, into London, via Baker Street and King's Cross, to Aldgate (for the City).

As its name suggests, the Metropolitan Line has its origins in its namesake railway company, the Metropolitan Railway. Having opened its initial stretch of line between Paddington and Farringdon in 1863, the first stretch of today's Metropolitan Line north of Baker Street was completed in 1868 as far as Swiss Cottage. This was followed by Swiss Cottage–West Hampstead 11 years later, and the line was then gradually extended northwards until Rickmansworth was reached in 1887, Chesham in 1889 and Amersham (along with the northernmost extensions to Aylesbury and Verney Junction) in 1892. The Harrow-on-the-Hill–Uxbridge branch opened in 1904 and Moor Park–Watford in 1925. Also served by the MR was the Brill branch but this never had a direct service to central London. From the 1910s onwards the entire area north of Baker Street served by the MR came to be known as Metroland.

Services to Verney Junction were withdrawn in 1936, and in 1961 the Metropolitan Line ceased to serve Aylesbury which has since been served only by trains from Marylebone on the remaining southernmost section of the erstwhile Great Central Main Line. These trains, operated by Chiltern Railways, have interchange with the Metropolitan Line at Amersham and Harrow-on-the-Hill, with LU and Chiltern sharing the same platforms at the intermediate stations at Chalfont & Latimer, Chorleywood and Rickmansworth. All of these stations are managed by London Underground, however.

As mentioned above, the Baker Street–Hammersmith line was also classed as part of the Metropolitan Line until 1990 when it was redesignated as the Hammersmith & City Line. Since then the Metropolitan Line has consisted entirely of the former MR lines north from Baker Street plus the top right-hand corner of the circle between Baker Street and Aldgate which is shared with Circle Line trains (and with the H&C as far as Liverpool Street).

The entire Metropolitan Line north of Finchley Road is above ground. Finchley Road–Baker Street–Aldgate is in tunnel apart from two short gaps at Farringdon and Barbican stations. Amersham is the highest station on the LU network at 147 metres above sea level, and the Metropolitan Line also has the longest distance between two LU stations: 6.3 km (4 miles) between Chesham and Chalfont & Latimer.

SERVICES

Historically, the Metropolitan Line has been a largely self-contained operation, with trains only continuing east of Baker Street in peak hours. Since 1990 trains have continued beyond Baker Street to Aldgate throughout the day, supplementing the Circle and Hammersmith & City Line trains on the northern part of the Circle Line and giving 30 trains per hour on the Baker Street–Liverpool Street section at peak times.

At present, off-peak Watford trains start and terminate at Baker Street, with most trains for Uxbridge and all those for Chesham and Amersham continuing to and from Aldgate. During peak hours the service pattern is more complex, consisting of a mixture of through trains to Aldgate and Baker Street terminators to and from all destinations.

Since December 2010, the Chesham branch has seen regular all-day through trains to and from Aldgate, having previously been served only by a shuttle from Chalfont & Latimer. This had the effect of halving the off-peak service frequency at Amersham from four to two trains per hour (although these are complemented by Chiltern Railways' two trains per hour London Marylebone–Aylesbury service), with the other two trains serving Chesham. Watford is served by four trains per hour and Uxbridge eight.

Another major change to the long-established service pattern was made in December 2011, with all trains calling at all stations between Finchley Road and Moor Park. Until that time, Watford trains ran semi-fast and Amersham trains were designated as "fast", but now only certain peak hour trains (a.m. peak southbound, p.m. peak northbound) pass non-stop through some stations. Trains classed as semi-fast are non-stop between Wembley Park and Harrow-on-the-Hill, with "fast" trains calling only at Harrow-on-the-Hill between Wembley Park and

Moor Park. Southbound fast and semi-fast trains in the morning peak do not call at Wembley Park.

An extension of the Watford branch to Watford Junction is planned, although at the time of going to press funding for this project, known as the Croxley Rail Link, is uncertain. If built, the scheme would involve the closure of the existing Metropolitan Line station at Watford and construction of a link between the LU branch and the DC Lines at Watford High Street with two new stations at Cassiobridge and Watford Vicarage Road. The expected opening date for the extension has been put back several times, and is currently forecast for 2020.

SUB-SURFACE LINE ROLLING STOCK AND DEPOTS

All Sub-Surface Line trains are now formed of S7 or S8 Stock built by Bombardier, Derby under the "Movia" marketing name. These trains are air-conditioned and all axles are powered. It is possible to walk through an entire train of S Stock, unlike other units which are formed of individual cars separated by emergency doors.

On the Metropolitan Line the S8s replaced the 1960s-built A Stock by 2012. The S8 Stock differs from the Circle, District and Hammersmith & City Line S7 Stock in having a mixture of facing and longitudinal seating. The S7 Stock replaced the 1960s/70s C Stock, the last of which was withdrawn in 2014 and also the D78 Stock. The last D78 stock was withdrawn from traffic just before this book closed for press in April 2017.

8-car (S8) trains are used on the Metropolitan Line only, 7-car (S7) trains are used on the Circle, District and Hammersmith & City lines. All S7 stock operates in a common user pool. All S Stock is in permanent formations and does not uncouple, including when lifted for depot examinations.

There were originally 58 S8 trains built. Also part of the Metropolitan Line fleet are two trains of S7 Stock that are formed as 8-car sets (known as S7+1 Stock, see note below). 50 trains are required for the Metropolitan Line peak service. The main depot for these is Neasden, trains also stable at Rickmansworth, Watford, Uxbridge, and Wembley Park.

In total there are 132 S7 trains. They entered service first on the Hammersmith & City Line in 2012, followed by the Circle Line and finally the District Line. The Circle and Hammersmith & City Lines are jointly managed, and 33 of the S7s are required for these two lines peak service. For maitenance purposes the S7s are based at the District Line depots at Ealing Common and Upminster, and can also receive attention at the Metropolitan Line depot at Neasden. For the Hammersmith & City and Circle the main depot for stabling is at Hammersmith, located adjacent to the H&C terminal bay platforms. Trains also stable at Ealing Common, Triangle Sidings (Gloucester Road), Wembley Park, Neasden, Edgware Road, Moorgate, Aldgate, Barking, and Upminster.

76 trains are required for the District Line peak service (unusually more are required in the evening peak compared to the morning peak (75 sets)). The main depots are at Ealing Common and Upminster; trains also stable at Richmond, Parsons Green, Lillie Bridge, Triangle Sidings, High Street Kensington, and Barking.

A note on the S7+1 sets: The original order for S Stock was for 133 7-car trains and 58 8-car trains (1395 vehicles). Later an additional train was added to the order to cover for an additional unit required to cover the Croxley extension. The additional train was built as a standard S7 unit (21567/568), tagged onto the end of the S7 build. However in order to create two additional trains for the Metropolitan Line (one for the Croxley link and another to provide an extra set for peak services) it was decided to augment two S7s to 8-cars (called S7+1). These were units 21323/324 and 21327/328, which were formed using the M2 vehicles from sets 21383/384 and 21385/386. New replacement vehicles were built for 21383/384 and 21385/386 (numbered 23384 and 23386). A quirk of these formations is that 21323/324 and 21327/328 (the two S7+1s) have two Sandite cars. This also means that two trains used only on the Metropolitan Line have all longitudinal seating, unlike the S8 Stock.

S STOCK

SUB-SURFACE LINES

Formations: S8: DM–M1–M2–MS–MS–M2–M1–DM.
S7: DM–M1–MS–MS–M2–M1–DM; S7+1: DM–M1–M2–MS–MS–M2–M1–DM.
Construction: Bolted and welded aluminium extrusions.
Traction Motors: 4 x AC fully suspended Bombardier MJB20093 of 65 kW (87 hp) per motor car.
Wheel Arrangement: Bo-Bo + Bo-Bo + Bo-Bo + Bo-Bo + Bo-Bo (+ Bo-Bo) + Bo-Bo + Bo-Bo.
Braking: Analogue rheostatic and regenerative.
Dimensions: 17.44/15.43 x 2.92 m. **Height:** 3.682 m.
Bogies: Flexible frame (Bombardier).
Gangways: Wide walk-through within unit; end emergency exit.
Couplers: LU automatic wedgelock with pneumatic connections.
Control System: IGBT.
Doors: Sliding plug.
Maximum Speed: S7: 45 mph; S8: 62 mph.
Train Protection: Tripcock but provisioned for Thales Seltrac CBTC.
Seating Layout: S7: 212 seats longitudinal, plus 44 tip-ups;
S7+1: 242 seats longitudinal, plus 50 tip-ups.
S8: 264 seats (some 2+2 facing one side, opposite longitudinal/tip-ups), plus 50 tip-ups.

Cars in the 25xxx number series are fitted with de-icing equipment.

S8 – 8-car units

DM. Bombardier 2008–12. 34 seats + 6 tip-ups. 33.3 tonnes.
M1. Bombardier 2008–12. 34 seats + 6 tip-ups. 30.6 tonnes.
M2. Bombardier 2008–12. 34 seats + 6 tip-ups. 27.5 tonnes.
MS. Bombardier 2008–12. 30 seats + 7 tip-ups. 29.2 tonnes.

DM	M1	M2	MS	MS	M2 †	M1	DM
21001	22001	23001	24001	24002	25002	22002	21002
21003	22003	23003	24003	24004	25004	22004	21004
21005	22005	23005	24005	24006	25006	22006	21006
21007	22007	23007	24007	24008	25008	22008	21008
21009	22009	23009	24009	24010	25010	22010	21010
21011	22011	23011	24011	24012	25012	22012	21012
21013	22013	23013	24013	24014	25014	22014	21014
21015	22015	23015	24015	24016	25016	22016	21016
21017	22017	23017	24017	24018	25018	22018	21018
21019	22019	23019	24019	24020	25020	22020	21020
21021	22021	23021	24021	24022	25022	22022	21022
21023	22023	23023	24023	24024	25024	22024	21024
21025	22025	23025	24025	24026	25026	22026	21026
21027	22027	23027	24027	24028	25028	22028	21028
21029	22029	23029	24029	24030	25030	22030	21030
21031	22031	23031	24031	24032	25032	22032	21032
21033	22033	23033	24033	24034	25034	22034	21034
21035	22035	23035	24035	24036	25036	22036	21036
21037	22037	23037	24037	24038	25038	22038	21038
21039	22039	23039	24039	24040	25040	22040	21040
21041	22041	23041	24041	24042	25042	22042	21042
21043	22043	23043	24043	24044	25044	22044	21044
21045	22045	23045	24045	24046	25046	22046	21046
21047	22047	23047	24047	24048	25048	22048	21048
21049	22049	23049	24049	24050	25050	22050	21050
21051	22051	23051	24051	24052	25052	22052	21052
21053	22053	23053	24053	24054	25054	22054	21054
21055	22055	23055	24055	24056	25056	22056	21056
21057	22057	23057	24057	24058	25058	22058	21058
21059	22059	23059	24059	24060	23060	22060	21060
21061	22061	23061	24061	24062	23062	22062	21062
21063	22063	23063	24063	24064	23064	22064	21064
21065	22065	23065	24065	24066	23066	22066	21066
21067	22067	23067	24067	24068	23068	22068	21068
21069	22069	23069	24069	24070	23070	22070	21070

▲ Metropolitan Line S8 Stock 21015/016 arrives at Harrow-on-the-Hill with a service for Aldgate on 11 May 2012. **Robert Pritchard**

▼ 21082/081 approaches Rayners Lane with a service for Uxbridge on 15 June 2016. **Robert Pritchard**

21071	22071	23071	24071	24072	23072	22072	21072
21073	22073	23073	24073	24074	23074	22074	21074
21075	22075	23075	24075	24076	23076	22076	21076
21077	22077	23077	24077	24078	23078	22078	21078
21079	22079	23079	24079	24080	23080	22080	21080
21081	22081	23081	24081	24082	23082	22082	21082
21083	22083	23083	24083	24084	23084	22084	21084
21085	22085	23085	24085	24086	23086	22086	21086
21087	22087	23087	24087	24088	23088	22088	21088
21089	22089	23089	24089	24090	23090	22090	21090
21091	22091	23091	24091	24092	23092	22092	21092
21093	22093	23093	24093	24094	23094	22094	21094
21095	22095	23095	24095	24096	23096	22096	21096
21097	22097	23097	24097	24098	23098	22098	21098
21099	22099	23099	24099	24100	23100	22100	21100
21101	22101	23101	24101	24102	23102	22102	21102
21103	22103	23103	24103	24104	23104	22104	21104
21105	22105	23105	24105	24106	23106	22106	21106
21107	22107	23107	24107	24108	23108	22108	21108
21109	22109	23109	24109	24110	23110	22110	21110
21111	22111	23111	24111	24112	23112	22112	21112
21113	22113	23113	24113	24114	23114	22114	21114
21115	22115	23115	24115	24116	23116	22116	21116

† De-icing vehicles (25xxx) are designated M2D.

Name:

21100 Tim O' Toole CBE

S7 – 7-car units (or * S7+1 8-car units)

DM. Bombardier 2011–15. 32 seats + 6 tip ups. 33.3 tonnes.
M1. Bombardier 2011–15. 30 seats + 6 tip-ups. 30.6 tonnes.
M2. Bombardier 2011–15. 30 seats + 6 tip-ups. 27.5 tonnes.
MS. Bombardier 2011–15. 29 seats + 7 tip-ups. 29.2 tonnes.

DM	M1	M2	MS	MS	M2 †	M1	DM	
21301	22301		24301	24302	25302	22302	21302	
21303	22303		24303	24304	25304	22304	21304	
21305	22305		24305	24306	25306	22306	21306	
21307	22307		24307	24308	25308	22308	21308	
21309	22309		24309	24310	25310	22310	21310	
21311	22311		24311	24312	25312	22312	21312	
21313	22313		24313	24314	25314	22314	21314	
21315	22315		24315	24316	25316	22316	21316	
21317	22317		24317	24318	25318	22318	21318	
21319	22319		24319	24320	25320	22320	21320	
21321	22321		24321	24322	25322	22322	21322	
21323	22323	25384	24323	24324	25324	22324	21324	*
21325	22325		24325	24326	25326	22326	21326	
21327	22327	25386	24327	24328	25328	22328	21328	*
21329	22329		24329	24330	25330	22330	21330	
21331	22331		24331	24332	25332	22332	21332	
21333	22333		24333	24334	25334	22334	21334	
21335	22335		24335	24336	25336	22336	21336	
21337	22337		24337	24338	25338	22338	21338	
21339	22339		24339	24340	25340	22340	21340	
21341	22341		24341	24342	25342	22342	21342	
21343	22343		24343	24344	25344	22344	21344	
21345	22345		24345	24346	25346	22346	21346	
21347	22347		24347	24348	25348	22348	21348	
21349	22349		24349	24350	25350	22350	21350	
21351	22351		24351	24352	25352	22352	21352	
21353	22353		24353	24354	25354	22354	21354	
21355	22355		24355	24356	25356	22356	21356	
21357	22357		24357	24358	25358	22358	21358	

▲ S8 Stock 21114/113 (for Uxbridge) overtakes Jubilee Line 96006/113 (for Stanmore) at West Hampstead on 5 July 2016. **Robert Pritchard**

21359	22359	24359	24360	25360	22360	21360
21361	22361	24361	24362	25362	22362	21362
21363	22363	24363	24364	25364	22364	21364
21365	22365	24365	24366	25366	22366	21366
21367	22367	24367	24368	25368	22368	21368
21369	22369	24369	24370	25370	22370	21370
21371	22371	24371	24372	25372	22372	21372
21373	22373	24373	24374	25374	22374	21374
21375	22375	24375	24376	25376	22376	21376
21377	22377	24377	24378	25378	22378	21378
21379	22379	24379	24380	25380	22380	21380
21381	22381	24381	24382	25382	22382	21382
21383	22383	24383	24384	23384	22384	21384
21385	22385	24385	24386	23386	22386	21386
21387	22387	24387	24388	23388	22388	21388
21389	22389	24389	24390	23390	22390	21390
21391	22391	24391	24392	23392	22392	21392
21393	22393	24393	24394	23394	22394	21394
21395	22395	24395	24396	23396	22396	21396
21397	22397	24397	24398	23398	22398	21398
21399	22399	24399	24400	23400	22400	21400
21401	22401	24401	24402	23402	22402	21402
21403	22403	24403	24404	23404	22404	21404
21405	22405	24405	24406	23406	22406	21406
21407	22407	24407	24408	23408	22408	21408
21409	22409	24409	24410	23410	22410	21410
21411	22411	24411	24412	23412	22412	21412
21413	22413	24413	24414	23414	22414	21414
21415	22415	24415	24416	23416	22416	21416
21417	22417	24417	24418	23418	22418	21418
21419	22419	24419	24420	23420	22420	21420
21421	22421	24421	24422	23422	22422	21422
21423	22423	24423	24424	23424	22424	21424
21425	22425	24425	24426	23426	22426	21426
21427	22427	24427	24428	23428	22428	21428
21429	22429	24429	24430	23430	22430	21430
21431	22431	24431	24432	23432	22432	21432
21433	22433	24433	24434	23434	22434	21434
21435	22435	24435	24436	23436	22436	21436
21437	22437	24437	24438	23438	22438	21438
21439	22439	24439	24440	23440	22440	21440
21441	22441	24441	24442	23442	22442	21442
21443	22443	24443	24444	23444	22444	21444
21445	22445	24445	24446	23446	22446	21446
21447	22447	24447	24448	23448	22448	21448
21449	22449	24449	24450	23450	22450	21450
21451	22451	24451	24452	23452	22452	21452
21453	22453	24453	24454	23454	22454	21454
21455	22455	24455	24456	23456	22456	21456
21457	22457	24457	24458	23458	22458	21458
21459	22459	24459	24460	23460	22460	21460
21461	22461	24461	24462	23462	22462	21462
21463	22463	24463	24464	23464	22464	21464
21465	22465	24465	24466	23466	22466	21466
21467	22467	24467	24468	23468	22468	21468
21469	22469	24469	24470	23470	22470	21470
21471	22471	24471	24472	23472	22472	21472
21473	22473	24473	24474	23474	22474	21474
21475	22475	24475	24476	23476	22476	21476
21477	22477	24477	24478	23478	22478	21478
21479	22479	24479	24480	23480	22480	21480
21481	22481	24481	24482	23482	22482	21482
21483	22483	24483	24484	23484	22484	21484
21485	22485	24485	24486	23486	22486	21486

21487	22487	24487	24488	23488	22488	21488
21489	22489	24489	24490	23490	22490	21490
21491	22491	24491	24492	23492	22492	21492
21493	22493	24493	24494	23494	22494	21494
21495	22495	24495	24496	23496	22496	21496
21497	22497	24497	24498	23498	22498	21498
21499	22499	24499	24500	23500	22500	21500
21501	22501	24501	24502	23502	22502	21502
21503	22503	24503	24504	23504	22504	21504
21505	22505	24505	24506	23506	22506	21506
21507	22507	24507	24508	23508	22508	21508
21509	22509	24509	24510	23510	22510	21510
21511	22511	24511	24512	23512	22512	21512
21513	22513	24513	24514	23514	22514	21514
21515	22515	24515	24516	23516	22516	21516
21517	22517	24517	24518	23518	22518	21518
21519	22519	24519	24520	23520	22520	21520
21521	22521	24521	24522	23522	22522	21522
21523	22523	24523	24524	23524	22524	21524
21525	22525	24525	24526	23526	22526	21526
21527	22527	24527	24528	23528	22528	21528
21529	22529	24529	24530	23530	22530	21530
21531	22531	24531	24532	23532	22532	21532
21533	22533	24533	24534	23534	22534	21534
21535	22535	24535	24536	23536	22536	21536
21537	22537	24537	24538	23538	22538	21538
21539	22539	24539	24540	23540	22540	21540
21541	22541	24541	24542	23542	22542	21542
21543	22543	24543	24544	23544	22544	21544
21545	22545	24545	24546	23546	22546	21546
21547	22547	24547	24548	23548	22548	21548
21549	22549	24549	24550	23550	22550	21550
21551	22551	24551	24552	23552	22552	21552
21553	22553	24553	24554	23554	22554	21554
21555	22555	24555	24556	23556	22556	21556
21557	22557	24557	24558	23558	22558	21558
21559	22559	24559	24560	23560	22560	21560
21561	22561	24561	24562	23562	22562	21562
21563	22563	24563	24564	23564	22564	21564
21565	22565	24565	24566	23566	22566	21566
21567	22567	24567	24568	23568	22568	21568

† De-icing vehicles (25xxx) are designated M2D.

▲ S7 Stock 21365/266 arrives at the easternmost station on the LU network, Upminster, on 9 October 2015. **Antony Guppy**

▼ Ealing Common depot has been upgraded for the new S7 Stock. In this 15 June 2016 view in the Middle shed, from left to right are 21504/503, 21357/358 and 21355/356. **Robert Pritchard**

1.9. NON-PASSENGER STOCK

This section contains details of former passenger carrying stock converted to departmental use and also engineering locomotives and purpose-built On-Track Machines.

Engineering trains operate on LU during the very limited hours when the network is not opened to passengers. Most trains are top-and-tailed by two of the battery electric locomotives. These normally travel from Ruislip depot to the worksite under electric power, then operate in battery power within a possession.

1.9.1. ENGINEERS' STOCK

RAIL ADHESION TRAINS   ex-A60 STOCK

These departmental Sandite units (nicknamed "RATS") are formed of two 4-car former Metropolitan Line A60 units, augmented to 5-car rail adhesion trains for Sandite dispersal on the Metropolitan Line with the addition of a third A60 Rail Adhesion Car. The spare cars are stored at Acton Works.

Formation: 5-car; DM–T–T–T–DM.
Construction: Aluminium body on steel and aluminium underframes.
Traction Motors: 4 x GEC LT114 of 48 kW (64 hp) per motor car.
Wheel Arrangement: Bo-Bo + 2-2 + 2-2 + 2-2 + Bo-Bo.
Dimensions: 16.17 x 2.95 m.
Bogies: Plate frame.
Control System: Resistor camshaft.

5110	6110	6036	6111	5111		5234	6234		6235	5235

Spare cars

5112	6112	6132	6113	5113

RAIL ADHESION TRAINS   ex-D78 STOCK

Two 4-car former District Line D78 units to be converted and augmented to 5-car rail adhesion trains (or "RATS") for Sandite dispersal, to replace the A60 Sandite units.

Formation: 5-car; DM–UNDM–T–UNDM–DM.
Construction: Aluminium body on aluminium underframe.
Traction Motors: 4 x DC nose-suspended Brush LT118 of 49 kW (60 hp) per motor car.
Wheel Arrangement: Bo-Bo + 2-2 + Bo-Bo + 2-2 + Bo-Bo.
Dimensions: 18.37/18.12 x 2.85 m.
Bogies: Box frame.
Control System: Resistor camshaft.

7010	8123	17010	8010	7123		7040	8107	17040	8040	7107

TRACK RECORDING TRAIN   ex-1960 & ex-1973 STOCK

3-car Track Recording Unit TRV (Track Recording Vehicle) formed of two former 1960 Stock motor cars either side of one former 1973 Stock trailer. Converted 1987 to monitor track condition.

Formation: 3-car; DM–T–DM.
Traction Motors: 4 x DC nose suspended GEC LT113 of 49 kW (60 hp) per motor car.
Wheel Arrangement: Bo-Bo + 2-2 + Bo-Bo.
Bogies: Plate frame.
Control System: Resistor camshaft.
Maximum Speed: 60 mph.

L132 ex-3901		TRC666 ex-514		L133 ex-3905

▲ The Metropolitan Line Sandite Unit (or "Rail Adhesion Train"), converted from A60 Stock 5110+6110+6036+6111+5111 passes Harrow-on-the-Hill heading north on 27 October 2016.
Kim Rennie

▼ Track Recording Train L132+TRC666+L133 passes Wimbledon Park, en route to Wimbledon on the District Line on 22 October 2013.
Robert Pritchard

RAIL ADHESION TRAINS & PILOT UNIT
ex-1962 and ex-1956 STOCK

Two Central Line Sandite units, one 8-car and one 5-car, plus a 4-car Stock Pilot Unit. 15 cars are adapted from 4-car 1962 Tube Stock plus two cars from similar 1956 Stock. The 1962 motor cars were built by Metropolitan-Cammell, the trailers by BR at Derby Works.

Formation: 8-car; DM–T–NDM–DM–DM–NDM–T–DM; 5-car; DM–NDM–T–NDM–DM; 4-car DM–T–NDM–DM.
Construction: Steel body on steel underframe.
Traction Motors: 2 x DC nose-suspended Brush LT112 of 60 kW (80 hp) per motor car.
Wheel Arrangement: 8-car; 1A-A1 + 2-2 + 1A-A1 + 1A-A1 + 1A-A1 + 1A-A1 + 2-2 + 1A-A1; 5-car; 1A-A1 + 1A-A1 + 2-2 + 1A-A1 + 1A-A1; 4-car 1A-A1 + 2-2 + 1A-A1 + 1A-A1.
Bogies: Plate frame.
Control System: Resistor camshaft.

*   Converted from 1956 Stock

1406	2682	9125*	1681	1682	9577	2406	1407	8-car Rail Adhesion Train
1560	2560	9561*	1561					4-car Pilot Unit
1570	9691	2440	9441	1441				5-car Rail Adhesion Train

ASSET INSPECTION TRAIN   ex-1967 and ex-1972 STOCK

Under protracted conversion into a new 3-car Asset Inspection Train to supplement, or eventually replace, the Track Recording Train. New numbers were not known at the time of going to press. Six vehicles have been reserved for possible conversion of two trains.

Formation: 3-car; DM–T–DM.
Construction: Aluminium body on steel underframe.
Traction Motors: 4 x DC nose-suspended Brush LT115 of 53 kW (71 hp) per motor car.
Wheel Arrangement: Bo-Bo + 2-2 + Bo-Bo.
Braking: Electro-pneumatic and rheostatic.
Dimensions: 16.09/15.98 x 2.64 m.
Bogies: Plate frame.
Control System: Resistor camshaft.

*   Converted from 1967 Stock (all others 1972 Stock).

3213	4213	3179*		3079*	4313	3313

FILMING UNIT   ex-1972 STOCK

4-car unit retained for movie filming purposes at Aldwych.

Formation: DM–T–T–DM.
Construction: Aluminium Body on steel underframe.
Traction Motors: 4 x DC nose-suspended Brush LT115 of 53 kW (71 hp) per motor car.
Wheel Arrangement: Bo-Bo + 2-2 + 2-2 + Bo-Bo.
Braking: Electro-pneumatic and rheostatic.
Dimensions: 16.09/15.98 x 2.64 m.
Bogies: Plate frame.
Gangways: Emergency end doors only.
Couplers: LU automatic wedgelock.
Control System: Resistor camshaft.
Doors: Sliding.
Maximum Speed: 45 mph.
Train Protection: Tripcock.

3229		4229		4329		3329

▲ The 5-car Rail Adhesion Train formed of 1962 Stock vehicles, led by 1570, passes the junction for West Ruislip and Ealing Broadway, towards the western end of the Central Line on 5 November 2015.
Alisdair Anderson

1.9.2. LOCOMOTIVES

SCHOMA DIESEL-HYDRAULIC or
*CLAYTON BATTERY LOCOMOTIVES   B or *Bo

Originally built to Tube gauge for construction of the Jubilee Line, then adsorbed into general engineers' stock. Built by Schoma in Germany as model CFL500VR diesel-hydraulic. Under conversion from 2014 onwards to *battery electric by Clayton. Rebuilt machines have two underframe mounted traction motors driving the former hydraulic transmission cardan shafts. Rebuilds are designated model CB40 by Clayton and have 120 tonne load haulage capacity.

All 12 are named after secretaries of works managers on the Jubilee Line extension project.

Built: 1996; * rebuilt 2014–
Builder: Schoma; * rebuilt by Clayton.
Engine: As built – MTU 6V183TD 370 kW (495 hp); * battery.
Transmission: As built – diesel-hydraulic, Voith; * electric.
Continuous Rating: 208 kW.
Length: 8.50 m.
Weight: As built: 33.9 tonnes; * 40.0 tonnes.
Maximum Speed: As built: 31 mph; * 19 mph.

B diesel-hydraulic locomotives or * Bo battery electric locomotives, rebuilt 2014 onwards

1	BRITTA LOTTA	6 *	DENISE	11 *	JOAN
2 *	NIKKI	7 *	ANNEMARIE	12	MELANIE
3	CLAIRE	8 *	EMMA	13 *	MICHELE
4 *	PAM	9	DEBORA	14 *	CAROL
5 *	SOPHIE	10 *	CLEMENTINE		

▲ Schoma diesel-hydraulic locomotives 1 "BRITTA LOTTA" and 3 "DENISE" at West Ruislip depot on 9 December 2015. **Keith Fender**

BATTERY ELECTRIC LOCOMOTIVES   Bo-Bo

These Tube gauge battery electric locomotives are based on a unique LT design first introduced in 1936. 52 were built to a similar basic design, but with each successive batch built up to 1974 incorporating progressive improvements (the 1985-built L62–L67 were unsuccessful and have since been scrapped). The 1936-built (L35–L43), 1951-built (L55–L61) and 1962-built (L76, later L33) batches are no longer in service. L35 is preserved (see section 2.4).

The underframes and bodies were newly built but traction motors and type Z bogies were recovered from passenger stock, except 1973 batch locomotives which have new bogies built to the old design. Batches were built for specific construction projects, then absorbed into general use.

Batteries are recharged at depots; there is no charging off traction rails. Battery capacity has been progressively increased over time from 768 Ah to 1008 Ah. All locos have tripcocks, but many are fitted with line specific train protection systems. Equipped with 3 mph slow speed control.

Privatisation placed all battery locomotives into TransPlant ownership, part of TubeLines, itself now a TfL subsidiary. All battery locomotives are now based at West Ruislip depot for both maintenance and operation. In 2010, a 15-year life extension and refurbishment of L24 was completed at Acton Works. L25 and L29 followed, and the remaining 26 should be done at a rate of four per year until early 2019. Refurbished locomotives are all fitted with new 168 cell Exide 1250 Ah batteries. Nominal traction rail voltage has been increased from 630 V to 750 V.

Current operations require 22 locomotives for weekends, based on 11 trains with one locomotive at each end. In addition to their L numbers, they carry a five digit number yy0xx, yy denoting year of build and xx the L serial number. Main line TOPS numbers were once allocated in the 970xx series, again with xx the L number; but they have long been deregistered. Further temporary numbers in the 977xx were allocated to some locomotives, also now deregistered, but all are shown here for completeness.

Built: p 1964; q 1969; r 1973.
Builder: p, q Metro-Cammell, Birmingham; r BREL Doncaster.
Battery: 1008 Ah (unrefurbished) or 1250 Ah (refurbished) lead acid.
Transmission: Electric or battery.
Traction Motors: 4 GEC WT54D of 112 kW continuous.
Maximum Tractive Effort: 17800 lbf (original build).
Continuous Rating: 600 hp (original build).
Length: 16.54 m (original build).
Weight: 53.8 tonnes (original build).
Wheel Diameter: 914 mm.
Maximum Speed: 30 mph.

c   Central Line ATP.
p   1969 batch originally delivered for final LT steam replacement.
q   1964 batch originally delivered for Victoria Line construction.
r   1973 batch originally delivered for Fleet Line and Heathrow construction.
t   Thales Seltrac TBTC.
v   Victoria Line ATP.
*   Refurbished from 2010 onwards.

L15	pt	69015	97015, 97715	L30	*qv	64030	97030
L16	*pt	69016	97016	L31	*qv	64031	97031
L17	*pt	69017	97017	L32	*qv	64032	97032, 97732
L18	*pt	69018	97018	L44	*rt	73044	97044
L19	*pt	69019	97019	L45	*rt	73045	97045
L20	qt	64020	97020, 97720	L46	*rt	73046	97046
L21	qt	64021	97021	L47	rt	73047	97047
L22	*q	64022	97022, 97722	L48	rt	73048	97048
L23	*q	64023	97023	L49	*rt	73049	97049
L24	*q	64024	97024	L50	*rt	73050	97050, 97750
L25	*q	64025	97025	L51	*rt	73051	97051, 97751
L26	*q	64026	97026	L52	rt	73052	97052, 97752
L27	*qv	64027	97027	L53	*rt	73053	97053, 97754
L28	*qv	64028	97028	L54	rt	73054	97054
L29	*qv	64029	97029				

▲ Battery-electric locomotive L26 on an engineers train at Paddington on 21 February 2010.
Tony Christie

▼ L28 and L24 (both refurbished) top-and-tail a new concrete mixing wagon at Northfields on 13 April 2016, after it had been tested on the South Ealing test track. **Kim Rennie**

1.9.3. ON-TRACK MACHINES

London Underground has a fleet of On-Track Machines operated through the Transplant business unit, all of which are based at Ruislip depot. These are used for maintaining, renewing and enhancing the network's infrastructure. Most machines are built to Tube profile, however the newer Tampers TMM774–TMM776 are built to Sub-Surface Line profile.

In addition other machines, particularly Rail Grinding Trains, are provided by specialist contractors for use on the network – some for lengthy periods – but these machines are not listed here.

CRANES

C623	Cowans Sheldon 7.5 tonne Light Duty Diesel Hydraulic	Built: 1982
C624	Cowans Sheldon 7.5 tonne Light Duty Diesel Hydraulic	Built: 1984
C625	Cowans Sheldon 7.5 tonne Light Duty Diesel Hydraulic	Built: 1984
C626	Cowans Sheldon 7.5 tonne Light Duty Diesel Hydraulic	Built: 1984

TWIN-JIB TRACK RELAYERS

TRM627	Cowans Boyd Self-propelled	Built: 1986
TRM628	Cowans Boyd Self-propelled	Built: 1993

TAMPERS

TMM771	Plasser & Theurer 07-16 Universal		Built: 1980
TMM772	Plasser & Theurer 07-16 Universal		Built: 1980
TMM773	Plasser & Theurer 07-16 Universal	"ALAN JENKINS"	Built: 1980
TMM774	Plasser & Theurer 08-275/4 ZW		Built: 2007
TMM775	Matisa B45UE	EVN 99 70 9128 003-9	Built: 2015
TMM776	Matisa B45UE	EVN 99 70 9128 004-7	Built: 2015

▲ Cowans Sheldon 7.5 tonne Light Duty Diesel Hydraulic Crane C623 is seen at Ruislip depot on 11 September 2012. **Kim Rennie**

▲ Plasser & Theurer 08-275/4 ZW Tamper TMM774 is seen at West Ealing on 5 April 2007.

Alex Hall

▼ New Matisa B45UE Tamper TMM776 in Ruislip depot on 21 July 2016.   **Kim Rennie**

2. PRESERVED UNDERGROUND STOCK

With a history dating back to 1863 it is not surprising that a number of former London Underground locomotives and trains are preserved at various museums and other private sites around the country.

The London Transport Museum's main site at Covent Garden houses a small number of preserved Underground vehicles, trams, buses and trolleybuses along with a collection of artefacts from London's transport system through the ages. Most of the museum's preserved vehicles reside at the London Transport Museum Depot at Acton which has two open weekends per year, usually in April and September. Guided tours of the depot are also available on a number of other dates throughout the year. Details of events and attractions at both sites can be found at www.ltmuseum.co.uk.

There are also a small number of preserved London Transport vehicles at various other sites such as Mangapps Railway Museum, Essex, and Buckinghamshire Railway Centre, Quainton Road. A few vehicles have even been converted for other uses, such as the D78 Stock car used as a library at Coopers Lane Primary School in Grove Park, South London and the 1983 Tube Stock cars in use as work rooms for artists and other creative practitioners at Village Underground on a part of the disused Broad Street viaduct in Shoreditch. A number of other vehicles are stored at private sites.

Some Underground stock is still used in passenger service – the most famous are the six 2-car 1938 Stock trains used by South West Trains on the Isle of Wight railway (detailed in other Platform 5 publications). Two 1959 Stock cars are also used as hauled stock in another unlikely location – the Alderney Railway in the Channel Islands.

Most preserved London Transport vehicles are on show as static exhibits only. However, a few of them are still in working order and are used on occasional special workings on the London Underground network, such as Metropolitan Railway steam locomotive No. 1, electric locomotive No. 12 "SARAH SIDDONS", and the 4-car train of 1938 Tube Stock based at the LT Museum's Acton depot. Other steam locomotives may also be used, and an ex-British Railways 4-car "4 TC" set is also based at London Underground's Ruislip depot for use as hauled stock (for details see the Platform 5 book "Preserved Locomotives of British Railways").

For a detailed list of locations see Appendix I.

2.1 METROPOLITAN RAILWAY STEAM LOCOMOTIVES

The Metropolitan Railway was a constituent of the present day London Underground Ltd, and is the only constituent company of LUL from which steam locomotives survive.

CLASS A   4-4-0T

Built: 1866 by Beyer Peacock.
Boiler Pressure: 120 lb/sq. in.   **Wheel Diameters:** 3' 0", 5' 9".
Cylinders: 17¼" x 24" (O).   **Weight:** 42.15 tons.
Valve Gear: Stephenson.   **Tractive Effort:** 12 680 lbf.

23–L45   London Transport Museum   BP 710/1866

BRILL BRANCH   4w WT

Built: 1872 by Aveling & Porter for use on Brill branch (Wotton Tramway).
Boiler Pressure: **Wheel Diameters:** 3' 0".
Cylinders: 7¾" x 10".   **Weight:**
Valve Gear: Stephenson.   **Tractive Effort:**

–   Buckinghamshire Railway Centre   AP 807/1872

CLASS E   0-4-4T

Built: 1898 at Neasden. 7 built.
Boiler Pressure: 150 lb/sq. in.   **Wheel Diameters:** 5' 6", 3' 9½".
Cylinders: 17¼" x 26" (I).   **Weight:** 54.5 tons.
Valve Gear: Stephenson.   **Tractive Effort:** 15 420 lbf.

1–L44   Buckinghamshire Railway Centre   Neasden 3/1898

2.2 LONDON UNDERGROUND DIESEL LOCOMOTIVES

London Underground Ltd has owned very few diesel locomotives, but two are now preserved.

UNCLASSIFIED   ROLLS–ROYCE   0-6-0

Built: 1967–68. 3 built. Acquired 1971 from Thomas Hill, Kilnhurst.
Engine: Rolls–Royce C8FL of 242 kW (325 hp).
Transmission: Hydraulic.
Maximum Tractive Effort: 128 kN (28 800 lbf). **Weight:** 48 tonnes.
Wheel Diameter: 1067 mm.

DL 82   Hardingham Station, Norfolk   RR 10272/1967
DL 83   Nene Valley Railway   RR 10271/1967

▲ Metropolitan Railway No. 1 is sometimes used on specials on the Underground. On 20 January 2013 it is seen at Farringdon with a special to celebrate 150 years of the Metropolitan Railway.
Alisdair Anderson

▼ Metropolitan Railway Class A 4-4-0T No. 23 is preserved at the London Transport Museum, Covent Garden, where it is seen on 11 May 2012. **Robert Pritchard**

2.3 LONDON UNDERGROUND ELECTRIC LOCOMOTIVES

CITY & SOUTH LONDON RAILWAY   Bo

Built: 1890 by Beyer-Peacock to Mather & Platt design. 14 built.
System: 500 V DC third rail system.   **Gauge:** 762 mm.
Maximum Tractive Effort: **Weight:** 10.3 tons.
Continuous Tractive Effort: **Wheel Diameter:** 686 mm.
Maximum Speed: **Continuous Rating:**

1–13   London Transport Museum   BP 1890

METROPOLITAN RAILWAY   Bo-Bo

Built: 1922–23. 20 built.   **Traction Motors:** Metropolitan Vickers MV339.
System: 630 V DC 4-rail system.   **Continuous Rating:** 895 kW (1200 hp).
Maximum Tractive Effort: 100 kN (22 600 lbf). **Weight:** 62.5 tons.
Continuous Tractive Effort: 65 kN (14 720 lbf). **Wheel Diameter:** 1105 mm.
Maximum Speed: 65 mph

5   JOHN HAMPDEN   London Transport Museum   VL 1922
12   SARAH SIDDONS   London Underground, Ruislip Depot   VL 1922

LONDON TRANSPORT EXECUTIVE   Bo-Bo

Built: Converted 1964 from two standard tube stock DM cars 3080+3109, built 1931 by Metropolitan-Cammell. Special purpose shunter for Acton Works internal use, created by cutting the DM cars in half and joining the two motor/cab ends together.
System: 630 V DC 4-rail system.
Traction Motors: 4 x GEC WT54 of 125 kW (167 hp).
Wheel Diameter: 915 mm.

L11   Cravens Heritage Trains, Epping   1964

LONDON PASSENGER TRANSPORT BOARD   Bo-2-2-Bo

Built: Converted 1940 at Acton Works from cars 3954 + 3995, originally Central London Railway cars 223 (Metropolitan-Cammell) and 265 (BRCW), built 1903. Sleet (de-icing locomotive); Inner bogies are non-load-bearing but carry de-icing equipment.
System: 630 V DC 4-rail system.   **Continuous Rating:**
Traction Motors: 4 x DC BTH GE66 of 93 kW (125 hp).
Maximum Tractive Effort: **Weight:** 41.45 tonnes.
Continuous Tractive Effort: **Wheel Diameter:** 890 mm.
Maximum Speed:

ESL 107   London Transport Depot Museum, Acton   1939

▲ Metropolitan Railway electric locomotive No. 12 "SARAH SIDDONS" is seen at Farringdon with a LT150 special on 20 January 2013. **Alisdair Anderson**

▼ London Transport Executive Bo-Bo electric shunting locomotive L11, formed of two converted standard Tube stock cars joined together, is owned by Cravens Heritage Trains and plinthed near Epping Station, where it is seen on 25 April 2015, as a Central Line train approaches on the adjacent running line. **Alan Yearsley**

▲ London Passenger Transport Board ESL 107 is seen at the London Transport Depot Museum at Acton on 26 September 2015. **Alisdair Anderson**

▼ London Electric Railways Standard Stock 3327, normally resident in the London Transport Depot Museum, was on display in Regent Street as part of TfL's Transport by Design display on 3 July 2016. **Kim Rennie**

2.4. BATTERY ELECTRIC LOCOMOTIVES

LONDON PASSENGER TRANSPORT BOARD   Bo-Bo

Built: 1938 by GRCW but mounted on former LT EMU bogies and uses former LT EMU traction motors. Operates off either battery or rail supply. 9 built.
Battery: 924 amp-hour capacity; 160 lead acid cells supplying 320 V.
Traction Motors: 4 x Metropolitan-Vickers MV145AZ of 113 kW (150 hp).
Weight: 54.6 tons.
Wheel Diameter: 940 mm.   **Maximum Tractive Effort:** 58 kN (17800 lbf).
Maximum Speed: 30 mph (rail supply), 15 mph (battery supply).

L35	London Transport Depot Museum, Acton	GRCW 1938

2.5. LONDON UNDERGROUND EMU STOCK

System: 630 V DC 4-rail system.

Q23 STOCK   DISTRICT RAILWAY

Built: Rebuilt 1935–40 from G Class stock, built 1923 for the District Railway.
Traction Motors: 2 x BTH GE69 of 149 kW (200 hp).

DM   15.77 x 2.62 m   29.5 tons   44 seats.

DR	*LER*	*LPTB*	*LTE*			
644	238	4148	4248	DM	London Transport Museum	GRCW 1923
662	274	4184		DM	London Transport Depot Museum, Acton	GRCW 1923

662 is currently stored at London Underground, Acton Works.

T STOCK   METROPOLITAN RAILWAY

Built: 1932 for the Metropolitan Railway. Converted 1961 for use as a sleet locomotive numbered ESL 118.
Traction Motors: 2 x GEC WT54 of 157 kW (210 hp).

DM   16.00 x 2.79 m   tons   50 seats.

MR	*LER*	*LPTB*	*LTE*			
249	2749	2749	ESL 118B	DM	Buckinghamshire Railway Centre	BRCW 1932
258	2758	2758	ESL 118A	DM	Buckinghamshire Railway Centre	BRCW 1932

STANDARD STOCK   LONDON ELECTRIC RAILWAYS

Built: 1923–35 for London Electric Railways. Those shown * were converted 1967 for the British Railways Isle of Wight Line.
Traction Motors: 2 x GEC WT54 of 112 kW (150 hp).

DM   16.70 x 2.60 m   29.5 tons   30 seats.
DT   15.70 x 2.60 m   19.0 tons   44 seats.
T   15.17 x 2.60 m   17.0 tons   48 seats.

LER	*LPTB*	*LTE*	*BR*			
297–3327	3327			DM	London Transport Depot Museum, Acton	MC 1927
320–3370	3370	L134		DM	London Transport Depot Museum, Acton	MC 1927
3693	3693	L131		DM	London Transport Depot Museum, Acton	MC 1934
1789–5279	5279*		27	DT	London Transport Depot Museum, Acton	MC 1925
846–7296	7296*		49	T	London Transport Depot Museum, Acton	CL 1923

Q35 STOCK LONDON PASSENGER TRANSPORT BOARD

Built: Rebuilt 1951 as Control Trailer from N Class stock, built 1936 for use on the Metropolitan Line Hammersmith–Barking section.

T 15.58 x 2.72 m tons 44 seats.

LPTB	LTE			
8063	08063	T	London Transport Depot Museum, Acton	MC 1936

CO/CP STOCK LONDON PASSENGER TRANSPORT BOARD

Built: 1938–39. CO Stock for the Hammersmith & City Line; CP Stock for the Metropolitan Line.
Traction Motors: 2 x MV145AZ of 113 kW (152 bhp).

DM 15.58 x 2.72 m tons 40 seats.
T 15.58 x 2.72 m tons 44 seats.

LPTB	LTE				
13028	53028	"CO"	DM	Buckinghamshire Railway Centre	BRCW 1938
013063	013063	"CO"	T	Buckinghamshire Railway Centre	GRCW 1938
14233	54233	"CP"	DM	Buckinghamshire Railway Centre	GRCW 1939
14256	54256	"CP"	DM	*Location unknown*	BRCW 1939

14256 is stored at an unknown location in Essex.

Q38 STOCK LONDON PASSENGER TRANSPORT BOARD

Built: 1938 for the Metropolitan Line.
Traction Motors: 2 x GEC WT45B of 113 kW (152 bhp).

DM 15.58 x 2.72 m tons 40 seats.

LPTB	LTE			
4416	L126	DM	London Transport Depot Museum, Acton	GRCW 1938
4417	L127	DM	London Transport Depot Museum, Acton	GRCW 1938

4416 is currently stored at London Underground, Acton Works.

1938 STOCK LONDON PASSENGER TRANSPORT BOARD

Built: 1938–40 for the Bakerloo, Northern and Piccadilly Lines.
Traction Motors: 2 x Crompton Parkinson/GEC/BTH LT100 of 125 kW (170 hp).

DM 15.93 x 2.69 m 27.40 tons 42 seats.
M 15.60 x 2.60 m 25.90 tons 40 seats.
T 15.60 x 2.60 m 20.70 tons 40 seats.

LPTB	LTE			
10012	10012	DM	London Transport Depot Museum, Acton	MC 1938
11178	11178–11012	DM	London Transport Depot Museum, Acton	MC 1938
11182	11182	DM	London Transport Museum	MC 1939
92048	92048–12048	M	London Transport Depot Museum, Acton	MC 1938
012229	012229–4927	T	Cravens Heritage Trains, Epping	BRCW 1938
012256	012256	T	London Transport Depot Museum, Acton	BRCW 1938

012229 is based at London Underground, Northfields Depot.

Six 2-car sets are in use with South West Trains on the Isle of Wight, details of these are given in other Platform 5 titles.

▲ The three CO/CP Stock cars, 53028, 013063 and 54233 are being restored at the Buckinghamshire Railway Central at Quainton Road, where they are seen on 5 August 2012.   **Alisdair Anderson**

▼ Operating a special in connection with the Rickmansworth Festival, 4-car 1938 Stock 10012, 012256, 12048 and 11012 is seen at Chalfont & Latimer with an Amersham–Harrow-on-the-Hill train on 19 May 2013. A number of this type of train are still used by South West Trains on the Isle of Wight railway.   **Alisdair Anderson**

R38 STOCK LONDON TRANSPORT EXECUTIVE

Built: 1938 as Q38 Stock (T). Rebuilt 1950 as R38 stock for the District Line (DM).
Traction Motors: 2 x DC LT 111 of 60 kW (80 hp).

DM   15.58 x 2.97 m   34.3 tons   ?? seats.

22624	DM	Mangapps Railway Museum	GRCW 1938

R49 SURFACE STOCK LONDON TRANSPORT EXECUTIVE

Built: 1951–53 for the District Line.
Traction Motors: 2 x LT 111 of 60 kW (80 hp).

DM   15.58 x 2.72 m   tonnes   40 seats.

LTE

21147	DM	Routemaster Heritage Centre, Hanwell	MC 1953
22679	DM	London Transport Depot Museum, Acton	MC 1952

1959 TUBE STOCK LONDON TRANSPORT EXECUTIVE

Built: 1959–61 for the Piccadilly Line.
Traction Motors: 2 x GEC LT112 of 60 kW (80 hp).

DM   15.98 x 2.60 m   26.62 tonnes   42 seats.

1018		DM	Woodlands, Coppleridge, Motcombe	MC 1959
1030		DM	Mangapps Railway Museum	MC 1959
1044		DM	Alderney Railway	MC 1959
1045		DM	Alderney Railway	MC 1959
1085	"1031"	DM	Alstom Train Services, Morden Depot	MC 1959
1304		DM	Woodlands, Coppleridge, Motcombe	MC 1961
1305		DM	Sutton Hall Railway, Rochford, Essex	MC 1961
2018		T	Woodlands, Coppleridge, Motcombe	MC 1959
2044		T	Mangapps Railway Museum	MC 1959
2304		T	Westfield Storage, Dinton, Wiltshire	MC 1959
9305		M	Westfield Storage, Dinton, Wiltshire	MC 1959

1960 TUBE STOCK LONDON TRANSPORT EXECUTIVE

Built: 1960. Prototype stock intended for the Central Line. The type never went into series production.
Traction Motors: 4 x DC nose suspended GEC LT113 of 49 kW (60 hp).

DM   15.86 x 2.60 m   29.89 tonnes   40 seats.

3906	DM	Cravens Heritage Trains, Epping	Cravens 1960
3907	DM	Cravens Heritage Trains, Epping	Cravens 1960

3906 and 3907 are based at London Underground, Northfields Depot.

A60 STOCK LONDON TRANSPORT EXECUTIVE

Built: 1960 for the Metropolitan Line.
Traction Motors: 2 x GEC LT114 of 48 kW (65 hp).

DM   16.17 x 2.95 m   31.60 tonnes   54 seats + 4 tip-ups.

5008–5034	DM	London Transport Depot Museum, Acton	Cravens 1961

▲ 1959 Stock DM 1085 (displaying false number 1031) is plinthed at the Alstom Northern Line depot at Morden, where it has been used as a classroom. It is seen on 26 November 2013.
Robert Pritchard

▼ As part of a special gala to commemorate 20 years since the cessation of LU services between Epping and Ongar, the preserved railway used 1960 Stock 3906 and 3907 (with 1938 Stock Trailer 4927 in the middle) on some services. They are seen at North Weald on 26 September 2014, being propelled by two Schoma locomotives.
Alisdair Anderson

1962 TUBE STOCK LONDON TRANSPORT EXECUTIVE

Built: 1962 for the Central Line.
Traction Motors: 2 x GEC LT112 of 60 kW (80 hp).

DM   15.90 x 2.60 m   26.62 tonnes   42 seats.
M   15.60 x 2.60 m   24.28 tonnes   40 seats.

1506	DM	Cravens Heritage Trains, Epping	BRCW 1962
1507	DM	Cravens Heritage Trains, Epping	BRCW 1962
2506	T	Cravens Heritage Trains, Epping	BRCW 1962
9507	M	Cravens Heritage Trains, Epping	BRCW 1962

1506, 1507, 2506 and 9507 are based at London Underground, Hainault Depot.

1967 TUBE STOCK LONDON TRANSPORT EXECUTIVE

Built: 1967–69 for the Victoria Line.
Traction Motors: 2 x Crompton Parkinson LT115 of 53 kW (70 hp).

DM   16.09 x 2.64 m   28.50 tonnes   40 seats.

3052	DM	London Transport Depot Museum, Acton	MC 1968
3122–3186	DM	Walthamstow Pumphouse Museum	MC 196?

1972 TUBE STOCK LONDON TRANSPORT EXECUTIVE

Built: 1972 for the Northern Line.
Traction Motors: 2 x Brush LT115 of 53 kW (70 hp).

DM   16.09 x 2.64 m   28.20 tonnes   40 seats.

3530	DM	London Transport Depot Museum, Acton	MC 1972
4079	T	*Location unknown*	MC 1972
4179	T	*Location unknown*	MC 1972

4079 and 4179 are owned by Village Underground, Shoreditch and are currently stored at an unknown location in Essex.

C77 STOCK LONDON TRANSPORT EXECUTIVE

Built: 1977 for the District Line.
Traction Motors: 2 x Brush LT117 of 68 kW (90 hp).

DM   16.03 x 2.92 m   31.70 tonnes   32 seats.

5721	DM	London Transport Depot Museum, Acton	MC 1977

D78 STOCK LONDON TRANSPORT EXECUTIVE

Built: 1979–83 for the District Line.
Traction Motors: 4 x DC nose-suspended Brush LT118 of 49 kW (65 hp) per motor car.

DM   18.37 x 2.85 m   27.4 tonnes   42 seats + 2 tip-ups.

7012	DM	London Transport Depot Museum, Acton	MC 19??
7027	DM	Coopers Lane Primary School, Grove Park	MC 19??

1983 TUBE STOCK   LONDON TRANSPORT EXECUTIVE

Built: 1983–88 for the Jubilee Line.
Traction Motors: 2 x Brush LT122 of 43 kW (55 hp).

DM   17.23 x 2.63 m   26.34 tonnes   48 seats.

3634	DM	Great Ormond Street Hospital, London	MC 1988
3662	DM	Village Underground, Shoreditch	MC 1988
3721	DM	Tyne & Wear Fire Service Training Centre, Washington	MC 1984
3733	DM	Village Underground, Shoreditch	MC 1988
3734	DM	London Transport Depot Museum, Acton	MC 1988
4633	T	Village Underground, Shoreditch	MC 1983
4662	T	Village Underground, Shoreditch	MC 1983

1986 PROTOTYPE TUBE STOCK
LONDON TRANSPORT EXECUTIVE

Built: 1986–87 for Central Line.
Traction Motors:

DM   16.85 x 2.75 m   tonnes   30 seats.

16	DM	London Transport Depot Museum, Acton	MC 1986

▲ A general view of the London Transport Museum Depot at Acton during an open weekend on 24 September 2016. Nearest the camera is prototype 1986 Tube Stock Driving Motor 16 on which the 1992 Stock was modelled. Next to it is 1972 Mark 1 Tube Stock DM 3530 (left) and LT Electric Sleet Locomotive ESL107 (right). Just visible in the background next to car 3530 is LT battery loco L35.   **Alan Yearsley**

2.6. SOUTHERN RAILWAY EMU STOCK

The following vehicle was not originally built for London Underground and was used on the Waterloo & City Line when it was operated by Southern Railway (and later BR).

CLASS 487   SOUTHERN RAILWAY W&C LINE

This vehicle is designated DMBSO – Driving Motor Brake Standard Open.

Built: 1940 for the Southern Railway Waterloo & City Line.
Traction Motors: 2 x EE 500 of 140 kW (185 hp).

DMBSO   14.33 x 2.64 m   29 tons   40 seats.

S 61 S – 61   DMBSO   London Transport Depot Museum, Acton   EE 1940

▲ Former Waterloo & City Line Class 487 DMBSO 61, in Network SouthEast livery, at the London Transport Depot Museum at Acton on 23 April 2016.   **Darren Ford**

3. UK LIGHT RAIL & METRO SYSTEMS

After a period of almost total abandonment in the decades following World War II, tramways have enjoyed a renaissance in the UK since the 1990s. This section contains details of the rolling stock fleets of all operational UK tram, light rail and metro systems (except the London Underground which is covered in a separate section). In addition to the seven tram networks, there are also three light metros in the UK: the Docklands Light Railway, the Glasgow Subway and the Tyne & Wear Metro. These are classed as metros rather than tramways because they run entirely on segregated rights of way rather than on-street. Heritage tramways such as those at Birkenhead and Seaton, and museum sites such as Beamish and Crich, are not included in this book. The heritage tram fleet at Blackpool has been included, however, as these vehicles are cleared to operate on a public tramway.

The UK had the honour of having the world's first passenger carrying railway, the Swansea & Mumbles Railway, opened to passengers in 1807. This was also the world's first passenger tramway because, although referred to as a railway it used tramway type vehicles throughout its life, starting with horse-drawn trams. It would be several more decades before other towns and cities followed suit, with the next horse tramway opening in 1860 in Birkenhead. Many more horse tramways followed in the latter part of the 19th century, and by the 1870s and 1880s some of these were beginning to give way to steam traction. The late 19th and early 20th century also saw some towns and cities such as Edinburgh and Matlock experiment with cable propelled tramways following the example set by San Francisco, USA, with its world famous cable tramway which opened in 1873. The Glasgow Subway also used the cable system from its opening in 1896 until 1935. Today, there are no surviving street running cable tramways in the UK apart from the Great Orme Tramway in Llandudno, North Wales. However, strictly speaking this is a funicular rather than a cable tramway, as the cars are stopped and started by stopping the cable, to which they are permanently fixed, unlike a cable tramway where the cable runs continuously and the cars can be attached to and detached from the cable. The Great Orme Tramway is not included in this book, as it is classed as a heritage/tourist tramway.

Blackpool was the UK's first electric tramway, opening in 1885 following earlier examples of electric traction in the early 1880s such as Sestroretsk in Russia, Lichterfelde, near Berlin, and the Mödling and Hinterbrühl Tram in Austria. Until 1899, Blackpool used a conduit electrification system whereby trams collected electric current from a conduit beneath the tracks via a groove between the two running rails. This system was also used on tram lines in central London, but soon proved to be unsuitable for Blackpool because the conduit was frequently damaged by sand and sea water, and it was replaced by overhead wires in 1899.

By the early 1900s, a small number of horse tramways had closed, but most had been converted to electric traction. This period also saw the opening of several completely new electric tramways, including many in small towns such as Merthyr Tydfil and Weston-super-Mare.

The heyday of the electric tram in the UK can perhaps best be described as having been between the 1900s and the 1920s. Sheerness & District Tramways was one of the shortest-lived tram systems in the country, running only from 1903 until 1917. Tramway closures began in earnest in the late 1920s, with several more small and medium-sized town networks being abandoned in the 1930s. By this time tramways were increasingly being replaced by buses and trolleybuses. Significant pre-war closures included Wolverhampton in 1928 and Nottingham in 1936.

After World War II, Manchester was the first major city to abandon its tram network in 1949, with almost all remaining systems succumbing during the 1950s such as Edinburgh in 1956, Liverpool in 1957, Aberdeen in 1958 (despite having introduced a new fleet of streamlined trams only 9 years earlier) and Leeds in 1959. By this time rising levels of car ownership and improvements in the design of motor buses meant that tramways were falling out of favour in the UK and in many other countries such as Canada, France, the USA and Australia. The last two tramway closures in the UK took place in Sheffield in 1960 and Glasgow in 1962, after which Blackpool became the sole surviving tramway in the country.

Increasing road congestion led the Government and local authorities to recognise the need for more radical public transport-based solutions. The UK's first modern light rail system was the Tyne & Wear Metro, opened in 1980, followed by the Docklands Light Railway in 1987. Manchester led the way in bringing trams back to the UK with the opening of its Metrolink system in 1992, and has since been joined by Sheffield, Birmingham, Croydon, Nottingham and Edinburgh. A number of other tramway schemes, including the Bristol and Leeds Supertram and Liverpool's Merseytram, have been proposed but abandoned.

Since their opening, the Manchester and Nottingham tramways have expanded considerably (as have the Docklands Light Railway and to a lesser extent the Tyne & Wear Metro) and are now much larger than their original networks, but those in Croydon, Sheffield and Edinburgh have so far remained unchanged. This was also the case with Birmingham's Midland Metro until recently, but a short extension into Birmingham city centre has now opened.

Despite the revival in the fortune of tramways in the UK in recent decades, only six new tram networks have so far opened. This is modest compared to some other European countries such as France where 22 new tramways have opened since the 1980s (with only three tram systems having operated continuously since opening in the late 19th century: Lille, Marseille and Saint-Étienne), starting with Nantes in 1985. There are also three French cities with rubber tyred vehicles guided by a single rail: Caen, Clermont-Ferrand and Nancy.

Trams have traditionally operated with a conductor who would issue and check tickets. Currently Birmingham, Blackpool and Sheffield trams have conductors, and on all other tramways and light rail networks tickets must be purchased before boarding and may be checked by ticket inspectors during the journey or when boarding or alighting. Information on ticketing and fares is included in the entry for each tramway.

To date, no two tram or light rail networks in the UK have used an exactly identical design of vehicle when first opening, with each system opting for a completely new design; however, Midland Metro's second fleet of trams, the CAF Urbos 3, is similar to those in Edinburgh. Also, many of the vehicle fleets are based on an existing design from abroad: London Tramlink's Bombardier Flexity Swift CR4000s are modelled on the K4000s in Cologne, Germany, and the Stadler Variobahns are similar to those used by Bybanen in Bergen, Norway. Similarly, Nottingham Express Transit's Bombardier Incentro AT6/5 was based on those built for Nantes, France.

▲ The newest section of tramway to open at the time of this book going to press was the Second City Crossing in Manchester, which opened to passengers on 26 February 2017. On the opening day, car 3112 heads away from the camera along Princess Street (past the Town Hall) before turning right onto Cross Street. It was working an East Didsbury–Rochdale service. **Robert Pritchard**

3.1. BLACKPOOL & FLEETWOOD TRAMWAY

Network: 11 miles.   **Lines:** 1.   **Depots:** 2 (Starr Gate and Rigby Road).   **First opened:** 1885.
www.blackpooltransport.com   **System:** 600 V DC overhead.
Standard livery: Flexity 2s and **F:** White, black & purple.

Until the opening of Manchester Metrolink, the Blackpool tramway was the only urban/inter-urban tramway system left in Britain. As mentioned in our Introduction, the seaside resort of Blackpool was the location for the UK's first electric tramway, opening on 29 September 1885 and operated by Blackpool Corporation from 1892. In 1898, the Blackpool & Fleetwood Tramroad Company opened a rival line between Gynn Square and Fleetwood Ferry. The two tramways were not connected until the Fleetwood line was taken over by Blackpool Corporation in 1920, enabling through running between South Shore and Fleetwood. By the 1920s there was an extensive network of street tramways to Layton, Squires Gate and Marton. These had all closed by 1962 so trams were concentrated on the Starr Gate–Fleetwood section. While all other UK tramways had closed by 1962, Blackpool stayed open, partly because of its unique value as a tourist attraction in its own right.

Today, Blackpool has a population of around 142 000. The tramway consists of a single route, 11 miles long, from the town of Fleetwood on the Fylde coast to the north of Blackpool, through Cleveleys and Bispham to Blackpool itself, where trams run along the promenade and beneath the famous Blackpool Tower, which is visible for miles around. After Pleasure Beach the line continues to the southern terminus at Starr Gate.

The Blackpool tramway is municipally operated by Blackpool Transport Services Ltd, which is owned by Blackpool Council and also runs buses in Blackpool. The infrastructure is owned by Blackpool Corporation.

After years of under-investment and a fleet of trams mainly dating from the 1930s, a decision was made in 2008 to upgrade the tramway to a modern light rail system, with new low-floor trams and rebuilt tracks and stops, at a cost of around £100 million. The system closed for upgrading in November 2011, and reopened in April 2012 with a new fleet of 16 Bombardier Flexity 2 trams: these are now used on the normal scheduled services. Part of the upgrade also included a new state-of-the-art depot at Starr Gate – the original depot at Rigby Road depot has been retained to maintain the "B" fleet (see below) and heritage trams.

The Heritage aspect of the operation has not been forgotten, and still brings in significant revenue for the tramway, especially the famous "illuminations tours" which operate every autumn in connection with the Blackpool Illuminations. The heritage side of the operation is operated by Blackpool Heritage Tram Tours, part of Blackpool Transport Services.

Today the fleet is split into three distinct fleets: The "A" fleet comprises 16 new Flexity cars used for the normal service. These Flexity 2 trams were built by Bombardier in Germany and are 5-section trams riding on three bogies, the two outer bogies being motored. They were delivered in 2011–12 and have a total capacity (standing and seating) of 200 passengers. Two further trams of this type (017 and 018) are on order for delivery in autumn 2017.

To supplement the Flexity service it was planned to retain and refurbish nine of the 1930s-built double-deck "Balloon" trams to operate a supplementary service between Pleasure Beach and Cleveleys at busy times. Nine Balloon cars were modified for this purpose and have a partial exemption from the Rail Vehicle Accessibility Regulations (RVAR) for use on normal services, forming the "B" fleet. This is because they have been made more accessible than in the past, and also on the basis that a fully compliant tram will always be available within 5 minutes of a "B" fleet car. The Balloons have been fitted with wide centre sliding plug doors to allow them to call at the rebuilt platforms. Despite the money spent on upgrading the fleet, the refurbished Balloon cars have seen little use, with the Flexity trams able to generally adequately cover the normal service and any extras required to operate. Only five of the refurbished Balloons were serviceable at the time of writing.

Finally the "C" fleet is the Heritage Fleet of Vintage cars, which have full exemption from the RVAR regulations to operate separate heritage, open-top or illuminated services. Initially there were planned to be 16 vehicles to form the core "C" fleet: Box car 40, Bolton 66, Standard 147, Open Boat cars, 600 and 602 and 604, Brush car 631, Centenary car 648, Corporation car 660, Progress twin-cars 672+682 and 675+685, Open-top Balloon 706, Balloon 717, Illuminated Western Train 733+734 (which is fitted with wheelchair access), Illuminated Warship 736, Illuminated Trawler 737. These have since been augmented by other former Blackpool trams

BLACKPOOL &
FLEETWOOD TRAMWAY

Fleetwood
Ferry
Victoria Street
London Street
Fisherman's Walk
Stanley Road
Lindel Road
Heathfield
Road
Broadwater
Rossall
Square
Rossall
School

Rossall Beach
Thornton Gate
West Drive
Cleveleys
Anchorsholme
Lane
Little Bispham
Norbreck North
Norbreck
Sandhurst
Avenue
Bispham
Cavendish Road
Lowther Avenue
Cabin
Cliffs Hotel
Gynn Square
Wilton Parade
Pleasant
Street
North Pier (nthbnd)
Future Spur to Blackpool North
North Pier (sthbnd)
Tower
Central Pier
Manchester
Square
*Rigby Road
Depot*
St Chad's Road
Waterloo Road
South Pier
Pleasure Beach
Burlington
Road West
Harrow Place
Starr Gate
*Starr Gate
Depot*

that have joined the fleet, and visitors from preserved tramways such as the National Tramway Museum at Crich or the North of England Open Air Museum at Beamish.

In terms of services, starting with the normal service, this operates either every 10 or 15 minutes during the day, depending on the time of year, with the journey from Fleetwood to Starr Gate timetabled to generally take 55 minutes. In the winter the service operates every 15 minutes between 08.00 and 19.00 (every 30/20 minutes in the early morning and every 30 minutes in the evening), requiring eight trams. In the peak season (April–October) the service runs every 10 minutes, generally requiring 13 trams. Additional short workings (such as Pleasure Beach–Little Bispham) can also operate at time of high demand.

The Heritage operation was scaled back for the 2014 and 2015 seasons on cost grounds, but expanded again in 2016 and 2017. Every weekend between late January and early November at least two cars from the heritage fleet are in operation between Pleasure Beach and Talbot Square (North Pier)/Cabin, operating to a frequent timetable (usually every 20/30 minutes between 10.00 and 17.00). The Heritage service also operates on weekdays during school holidays and every day in July and August and between mid October and early November. Once a month an enhanced "Gold" heritage services operates (often on Bank Holiday weekends) with six or more heritage trams in operation, including trips the full length of the line to Fleetwood. Dates of these weekends are published on the Blackpool transport website or at the dedicated Heritage operation site – www.blackpoolheritage.com. The Heritage services call at slightly different stops from normal services – there are six that can be served by the Heritage services (Pleasure Beach, Tower/North Pier, Cabin, Bispham, Cleveleys and Fleetwood).

During the illuminations season (early September until early November) tram tours using Heritage or Illuminated vehicles operate from Pleasure Beach to Bispham from dusk every evening. Boarding of these special trips is only allowed at Pleasure Beach, but passengers may alight on the return at Bispham, Cabin or Tower/North Pier. A Heritage day ticket is valid to travel on the Illuminations tours.

It should be noted that unlike the other tramways listed in this book Blackpool operates from a lower voltage – of 600 V DC. This was increased from 550 when the tramway was upgraded in 2011–12. Trams are restricted to 30 km/h (around 19 mph) along the promenade as far as Cabin, and also through the streets of Fleetwood.

Tickets can be purchased from conductors on the trams in the time-honoured way. Single fares start from £1.60. One day "Blackpool1" tickets valid on buses and trams in Blackpool cost £5 (£4.50 if bought from a PayPoint shop). 24 hour or 3 or 7 day tickets are also available. A Heritage ticket giving day travel on the heritage services (if operating) as well as the normal tram and bus services costs £11 and can be bought on board heritage tram services or on normal service trams. A round-trip ticket for use on the heritage trams is also available for £3.50.

According to the Department for Transport annual light rail usage figures Blackpool trams carried 4.9 million passengers in 2015–16. This illustrates the success of the upgraded tramway and the enhanced capacity the Flexity trams provide, being the highest figure for more than 20 years, and also an increase of more than 20% on the previous year. These figures exclude passengers carried on the heritage services, which are counted separately.

It is planned to extend the tramway from North Pier up Talbot Road to Blackpool North station, with work due to start in 2018 and the extension opening in spring 2019. Two new Flexity trams have been ordered for this extension, and will initially be used on the existing system. Another possible future extension would be from Starr Gate to the Airport.

▲ The 16 Bombardier Flexity 2 trams operate the core service in Blackpool. On 5 November 2016 002 leaves the Fleetwood Ferry terminus on its way back to Starr Gate. **Robert Pritchard**

▼ On 27 October 2012 014 arrives at Bispham with a Fleetwood–Starr Gate service.
Robert Pritchard

FLEXITY 2   "A FLEET"   5-SECTION TRAMS

The Flexity 2 trams operate normal scheduled services. 017 and 018 are on order.
Built: 2011–12 by Bombardier Transportation, Bautzen, Germany.
Wheel Arrangement: Bo-2-Bo.
Traction Motors: 4 x Bombardier 3-phase asynchronous of 120 kW (161 hp).
Seats: 70 (+4).   **Weight:** 40.9 tonnes.
Dimensions: 32.20 x 2.65 m.   **Doors:** Sliding plug.
Braking: Regenerative, disc and magnetic track.
Couplers: **Maximum Speed:** 43 mph.
Advertising Livery: 016 Fleetwood Freeport (blue).

001	005	009	013	016 **AL**
002	006	010	014	017
003	007	011	015	018
004	008	012		

Names:

002	Alderman E.E. Wynne		007	Alan Whitbread

"BALLOON" DOUBLE DECKERS   "B FLEET"   A1-1A

The nine cars listed have partial exemption from the Rail Vehicle Accessibility Regulations (RVAR) and have been fitted with wider doors. They see limited use, often during the autumn illuminations season or in high summer. They are also sometimes used on Heritage tours.

Built: 1934–35 by English Electric, Preston.
Traction Motors: 2 x EE305 of 40 kW (53 hp).   **Seats:** 94 (*† 92).
Advertising Liveries: 707: Coral Island: The Jewel on the Mile (black).
                   709: Blackpool Sealife Centre (blue).
                   713: Houndshill Shopping Centre (purple & white).
                   720: Walls ice cream (red).
                   724: Lyndene Hotel (blue).
*   Rebuilt with a flat front end design and air-conditioned cabs.

700		**F**	711	†	**F**	719		**F**
707	*	**AL** (S)	713		**AL**	720		**AL** (S)
709	*	**AL** (S)	718	*	**Green/cream**	724	*	**AL** (S)

Names:

711	Ray Roberts		719	Donna's Dream House

HERITAGE FLEET of VINTAGE CARS "C FLEET"

The following trams have exemption from the Rail Vehicle Access Regulations (RVAR) for Heritage use. They normally see use on the weekend heritage trips, during the autumn Illuminations season or for private excursions. Some vehicles are undergoing restoration.

Blackpool & Fleetwood 40[1]	Single-deck Fleetwood Box car	Built: 1914
Bolton 66[2]	Bogie double-decker	Built: 1901
Blackpool 147 "MICHAEL AIREY"	Standard double-decker	Built: 1924
Blackpool 225–600 "THE DUCHESS OF CORNWALL"	Open boat car	Built: 1934
Blackpool 227–602	Open boat car	Built: 1934
Blackpool 230–604 "GEORGE FORMBY OBE"	Open boat car	Built: 1934
Blackpool 294–631	Brush Railcoach	Built: 1937
Blackpool 304–641 (S)	Coronation Class single-decker	Built: 1952
Blackpool 642	Centenary car	Built: 1986
Blackpool 648	Centenary car	Built: 1985
Blackpool 272+T2–672+682	Progress Twin Car	Rebuilt: 1960
Blackpool 275+T5–675+685	Progress Twin Car	Rebuilt: 1958/60
Blackpool 280–680[3]	English Electric Railcoach	Rebuilt: 1960

▲ Blackpool & Fleetwood box car 40, part of the National Tramway Museum collection, is a regular on the Heritage services. On 5 November 2016 it runs along the promenade, passing the famous Tower, for Talbot Square (North Pier). **Robert Pritchard**

▼ Balloon double-deck car 701 is seen in the turning circle at Pleasure Beach before leaving with a service to Little Bispham on 17 April 2017. **Alisdair Anderson**

Blackpool 238–701	Balloon double-decker	Built: 1934
Blackpool 240–703	Balloon double-decker	Built: 1934
Blackpool 243–706 "PRINCESS ALICE"	Balloon open-top double-decker	Built: 1934
Blackpool 252–715	Balloon double-decker	Built: 1935
Blackpool 254–717 "WALTER LUFF"	Balloon double-decker	Built: 1935
Blackpool 260–723	Balloon double-decker	Built: 1935

Illuminated cars

Blackpool 733	Western Train loco & tender	Rebuilt: 1962
Blackpool 734	Western Train carriage	Rebuilt: 1962
Blackpool 736	"Frigate" HMS Blackpool	Rebuilt: 1965
Blackpool 737	"Fisherman's Friend" Illuminated Trawler	Rebuilt: 2001

[1] On long-term lease from the National Tramway Museum, Crich.
[2] Owned by the Bolton 66 Tramcar Trust.
[2] On loan from the Manchester Transport Museum Society, Heaton Park Tramway.

STORED VEHICLES

The following Heritage vehicles are currently stored at Rigby Road depot.

Blackpool 8	BCT One Man Car	Rebuilt: 1974
Lytham 43	English Electric double-deck open balcony car	Built: 1924
Blackpool 143	Standard double-decker	Built: 1924
Blackpool 279–679	English Electric Railcoach (ex-Twin Car motor)	Rebuilt: 1960
Blackpool 287–259–624	Brush Railcoach	Built: 1937
Blackpool 290–627	Brush Railcoach	Built: 1937
Blackpool 284–621	Brush Railcoach	Built: 1937
Blackpool 295–632	Brush Railcoach	Built: 1937
Blackpool 297–634	Brush Railcoach	Built: 1937
Blackpool 324–660	Coronation Class single-decker	Built: 1953
Blackpool 327–663	Coronation Class single-decker	Built: 1954
Blackpool 271+T1–671+681	Progress Twin Car	Rebuilt: 1960
Blackpool 276+T6–676+686	Progress Twin Car	Rebuilt: 1958/60
Blackpool 241–704	Balloon double-decker	Built: 1934
Blackpool 245–708	Balloon double-decker	Built: 1934
Blackpool 168–732	Rocket illuminated car	Built: 1961
Blackpool 222–735	Hovertram illuminated car	Rebuilt: 1963
Blackpool 761	Jubilee Class double-decker	Rebuilt: 1979

ENGINEERING CAR

Built: 1992 as a purpose-built overhead line engineering car for Blackpool Transport, the first completely new works car on the system. Fitted with an inspection platform.

754

▲ The fantastic Illuminated Western Train loco & tender (733) and Western Train coach (734) are used to give tours of Illuminations every autumn. On 5 November 2016 733+734 loads with passengers at Pleasure Beach. Behind is "Frigate" HMS Blackpool 736. **Robert Pritchard**

▼ Engineering car 754 hauls the failed Blackpool & Fleetwood box car 40 back to the depot at North Pier on 20 June 2015. This is the location from where the new extension will run to North station (note the points are already laid). **Alan Yearsley**

3.2. DOCKLANDS LIGHT RAILWAY

Network: 23½ miles. **Lines:** 6. **Depots:** 2 (Beckton and Poplar). **First opened:** 1987.
www.tfl.gov.uk/dlr **System:** 750 V DC third rail (bottom contact).

The unique Docklands Light Railway in east London is a driverless Metro where trains are normally driven automatically using the Thales Seltrac moving block signalling system. They can also be driven manually by the "Passenger Service Agent", the member of staff present on every train.

First conceived in 1981 as a link between the city of London and new offices in the regenerated Isle of Dogs and Canary Wharf areas, the first part of the DLR system opened in summer 1987 with two routes. One linked Tower Gateway (close to Fenchurch Street) with Island Gardens via Canary Wharf, while the other ran from Stratford to Island Gardens. This initial network of 8 miles with 15 stations used just 11 of the original P86 trains, running singly. These were joined by ten P89 trains in 1989. The original routes were largely on old railway routes, with Tower Gateway–Island Gardens mostly on viaducts, while the later extensions have mostly new formations. Platforms were soon extended and 2-car operation started in 1991 when the first of the B90 cars were delivered.

Originally owned by London Transport, DLR is now part of the London Rail division of Transport for London (TfL), operated by a consortium of Keolis and Amey on behalf of TfL. KeolisAmey Docklands is contracted to run DLR from December 2014 to April 2021 with the option for this to be extended to 2023. KeolisAmey took over from Serco, which had operated DLR since 1997.

In the 30 years since opening DLR has gone from strength to strength and is now an integral part of the London public transport network. With 149 trains compared to 11 when it opened, it runs between two termini in central London, at Bank and Tower Gateway, to Lewisham, Stratford/ Stratford International, Beckton and Woolwich Arsenal.

The dates of the numerous extensions are given below. Some of these lines used former railway alignments. Tower Gateway proved inadequate as a London terminus and a new underground station at Bank (accessed via twin tunnels and a 1 in 17 gradient), more convenient for onward Underground connections and the city of London, opened in 1991. The 1994 extension to Beckton made extensive use of viaducts and also serves the ExCel exhibition centre and gives access to a new second depot, relieving pressure on the original cramped depot at Poplar.

A further extension south to Lewisham 5 years later saw DLR cross to the southern side of the River Thames for the first time. The original elevated Island Gardens station was replaced with a new sub-surface station when the Lewisham extension opened. In the 2000s Woolwich Arsenal, via London City Airport and a second crossing of the river was reached via an extension from Canning Town. The Stratford International route partly replaced former North London Line services between Canning Town and Stratford. Opening dates for the DLR lines are as follows:

31 August 1987: Tower Gateway–Island Gardens/Poplar–Stratford;
29 July 1991: Shadwell–Bank;
28 March 1994: Poplar–Beckton;
20 November 1999: Island Gardens–Lewisham;
2 December 2005: Canning Town–King George V;
10 January 2009: King George V–Woolwich Arsenal;
31 August 2011: Canning Town–Stratford–Stratford International.

Today DLR has 45 stations. Despite the different routes, route numbers or colours are not used. Services are very frequent across the network, combining to give a train every 2 minutes at peak times on the very busy Limehouse–Shadwell section (every 2½ minutes off-peak). Details of the different routes and their frequency on weekdays is given below:

Bank–Canary Wharf–Lewisham: Every 5 minutes/4 minutes (peak). Journey time 25 minutes;
Bank–Poplar–Woolwich Arsenal: Every 10 minutes/8 minutes (peak). Journey time 26 minutes;
Tower Gateway–Poplar–Beckton: Every 10 minutes/8 minutes (peak). Journey time 26 minutes;
Stratford Int–Canning Town–Woolwich Arsenal: Every 10 min/8 min (peak). Journey time 23 min;
Stratford–Poplar–Canary Wharf*: Every 5 minutes/4 minutes (peak). Journey time 12 minutes;
Canning Town–Beckton: Every 10 minutes (off-peak). Journey time 13 minutes.
*   Extended to Lewisham in the morning peak.

All services normally use 3-car sets, except Stratford–Canary Wharf/Lewisham, Stratford International–Woolwich Arsenal and the off-peak Canning Town–Beckton shuttle which use 2-cars.

DOCKLANDS LIGHT RAILWAY

▲ A typical Docklands Light Railway scene as B90 and B92 cars 28+47 arrive at the elevated station of Blackwall with a service for Tower Gateway on 14 August 2016. **Robert Pritchard**

▼ B92 Class car 91 brings up the rear of a 3-train Stratford International service at Stratford (low level) station on 27 May 2013. **Antony Guppy**

Trains run from around 05.30 to midnight. An unusual quirk of the timetable is that the Canning Town–Beckton section has a more frequent service in the off-peak than the peak timetable (every 5 minutes off-peak but every 8 minutes peak).

Rather like London Underground stock, the DLR rolling stock class designations (ie "P86") denote the year that class of stock was first designed. The different types of stock are technically very similar, although the newest, B2007 cars look rather different. All trains are articulated 2-car sets, although referred to by DLR as one train. The oldest trains were built by BN Construction of Belgium (a company later taken over by Bombardier). As they were not suitable for underground operation (to Bank), the original P86 and P89 Class vehicles 01–21 were withdrawn from service in 1991 (01–11) and 1995 (12–21) and are now used by the Metro in Essen, Germany. 23 similar B90 cars were delivered in 1991–92, and were followed by 47 B92 cars in 1992–95 – principally for the Beckton extension. The final cars built to the original design were 24 Class B2K cars built 2002–03 (numbered 92–16 these duplicate some of the numbers of the original cars). These were built by Bombardier in Belgium. B90, B92 and B2K cars can all operate with each other, but not with the newer B2007 cars. The vehicles all have a floor height of 1025 mm above rail level and provide step-free access.

To enable 3-car operation 55 more cars were ordered from Bombardier. Called B2007 cars these entered traffic between 2008 and 2010. Technically they are very similar to the earlier cars, being 2-section units with motor bogies at each end. They were built by Bombardier at its Bautzen plant in Germany. 3-train operation started from February 2010, initially between Bank and Lewisham, and now most trains are formed of three units. In 2015 the seating layout in the B2007s was changed to mostly longitudinal (inwards facing) Tube style seating, to create more standing room.

The original livery was blue, red and white. This was replaced from 2004 by a mainly red livery, with a curving blue stripe to represent the River Thames.

The current timetable requires 134 of the 149 units in service, with nominally 140 available for service (with two 3-car "hot spare" trains). There are two depots, the large depot and stabling sidings at Beckton, plus the original depot and workshops at Poplar. At Poplar a diesel-hydraulic shunting locomotive and battery electric works locomotive are based at the depot. The DLR control centre is located at Beckton.

All trains are staffed by Passenger Service Agents, who are responsible for closing the doors and also checking tickets. DLR forms part of the TfL network, with interchange available at many places with London Underground or heavy rail, the main interchanges being at Bank, West Ham, Canning Town, Stratford, Woolwich Arsenal and Lewisham. A single with Oyster smartcard costs from £2.40 and with a paper ticket from £4.90. A Zones 1–4 Travelcard is valid on the whole of the DLR network. The system is generally "open", most stations not having ticket gates, but tickets must be purchased before boarding trains.

Given the size of today's network there is not one place where all trains can be seen; however, Poplar is a good location for observing services – and those trains not serving the station can be seen on the viaduct near West India Quay station, so all but trains on the Stratford International– Woolwich and Canning Town–Beckton routes can be seen. For the services running into Tower Gateway and Bank, Shadwell is a good station for observing – and c2c services can also be seen on the adjacent main line. Given the fact that it is largely elevated, DLR has become something of a tourist attraction in its own right, thanks to the fine views that can be had of the changing London landscape – especially from the front windows. DLR also allows easy access to the Emirates Airline cableway, the north bank terminus being close to the Royal Victoria stop.

DLR carried 116.9 million passengers in 2015–16, patronage having increased by 40% in the last 4 years. It is projected to grow by a further 38% by 2024. There are no extensions imminently planned, the proposed Dagenham Dock line now planned to be constructed as a London Overground link to Barking Riverside. However, in late 2016 Mayor of London Sadiq Khan instructed TfL to take forward a new extension of DLR from Gallions Reach (on the Beckton branch) to Thamesmead. This would cross the Thames and help support new housing developments to the north of Woolwich.

In 2015 DLR began an industry consultation on a possible new generation of rolling stock to continue to meet the growth in passenger numbers. Replacement of all 94 B90/B92/B2K trains is under consideration (although the B2K trains only date from 2002–03). While like-for-like replacement is not ruled out, between 40 and 50 new fixed formation trains without intermediate cabs are considered more likely, featuring wider doors and more standing room. New trains would also enable more services to operate on the Beckton line. It is expected that any new rolling stock would be introduced in the early 2020s.

CLASS B90   2-SECTION UNITS

Built: 1991–92 by BN Construction, Bruges, Belgium. Chopper control.
Wheel Arrangement: B-2-B.   **Traction Motors:** 2 x Brush DC 140 kW (187 hp).
Seats: 52 (+4).   **Weight:** 36 tonnes.
Dimensions: 28.80 x 2.65 m.   **Braking:** Rheostatic and regenerative.
Couplers: Scharfenberg.   **Maximum Speed:** 50 mph.
Doors: Sliding. End doors for staff use.

22	27	32	37	41
23	28	33	38	42
24	29	34	39	43
25	30	35	40	44
26	31	36		

CLASS B92   2-SECTION UNITS

Built: 1992–95 by BN Construction, Bruges, Belgium. Chopper control.
Wheel Arrangement: B-2-B.   **Traction Motors:** 2 x Brush DC 140 kW (187 hp).
Seats: 52 (+4).   **Weight:** 36 tonnes.
Dimensions: 28.80 x 2.65 m.   **Braking:** Rheostatic and regenerative.
Couplers: Scharfenberg.   **Maximum Speed:** 50 mph.
Doors: Sliding. End doors for staff use.

45	55	65	74	83
46	56	66	75	84
47	57	67	76	85
48	58	68	77	86
49	59	69	78	87
50	60	70	79	88
51	61	71	80	89
52	62	72	81	90
53	63	73	82	91
54	64			

CLASS B2K   2-SECTION UNITS

Built: 2002–03 by Bombardier Transportation, Bruges, Belgium.
Wheel Arrangement: B-2-B.   **Traction Motors:** 2 x Brush DC 140 kW (187 hp).
Seats: 52 (+4).   **Weight:** 36 tonnes.
Dimensions: 28.80 x 2.65 m.   **Braking:** Rheostatic and regenerative.
Couplers: Scharfenberg.   **Maximum Speed:** 50 mph.
Doors: Sliding. End doors for staff use.

92	97	03	08	13
93	98	04	09	14
94	99	05	10	15
95	01	06	11	16
96	02	07	12	

▲ A classic DLR setting, as a 3-car set of B92 stock led by 65 passes Limehouse Basin en route to Bank on 16 February 2017.   **Chris Booth**

CLASS B2007 2-SECTION UNITS

Built: 2007–10 by Bombardier Transportation, Bautzen, Germany.
Wheel Arrangement: B-2-B.
Seats: 52 (+4).
Dimensions: 28.80 x 2.65 m.
Couplers: Scharfenberg.
Doors: Sliding. End doors for staff use.

Traction Motors: 4 x VEM AC 130 kW (174 hp).
Weight: 38.2 tonnes.
Braking: Rheostatic and regenerative.
Maximum Speed: 50 mph.

101	112	123	134	145
102	113	124	135	146
103	114	125	136	147
104	115	126	137	148
105	116	127	138	149
106	117	128	139	150
107	118	129	140	151
108	119	130	141	152
109	120	131	142	153
110	121	132	143	154
111	122	133	144	155

CT30 DIESEL MECHANICAL CRANE TROLLEY

Built: 1986 by Wickham. Hertfordshire. Used for shunting, or for maintenance of overhead or lineside structures. Works No. 11622.
Engine: Ford Sabre 6 cylinder.
Dimensions: 6.75 x 2.63 m.
Weight: 8.25 tonnes.

Wheel Arrangement: Bo.

Maximum Speed: 25 mph.

992

BATTERY ELECTRIC WORKS LOCOMOTIVE WITH CRANE

Built: 1991 by RFS Industries, Kilnhurst, rebuilt 2014 by Hunslet Engine Company Ltd, Leeds.
Battery: Oldham Compton 750 V DC (fully charged).
Traction Motors: 1 x 150 kW.
Dimensions: 7.55 x 2.50 m.
Weight: 22 tonnes.

Wheel Arrangement: B.

Maximum Speed: 12 mph.

993 KYLIE

DIESEL-HYDRAULIC SHUNTING LOCOMOTIVE

Built: 1979 by GEC Traction Ltd, Vulcan Foundry, Newton-le-Willows. One of three locomotives originally built for Shotton steelworks.
Wheel Arrangement: B.
Engine: Gardner 6LXB 165 bhp.
Dimensions: 6.48 x 2.59 m.
Weight: 20 tonnes.

Maximum Speed: 16 mph.

994 KEVIN KEANEY

▲ B2K and B92 cars 96, 62 and 77 are seen undergoing maintenance in the principal depot at Beckton on 7 April 2017. **Robert Pritchard**

▼ B2007 cars 154 and 124 pass the other depot at Poplar with an empty stock move from the depot, to enter service for the evening peak on 7 April 2017. **Robert Pritchard**

▲ B2007 Class cars 155+120 arrive at Bow Church with a Stratford–Canary Wharf service on 16 September 2010. **Robert Pritchard**

▼ DLR 0-4-0 Diesel Hydraulic GEC shunter 994 "KEVIN KEANEY" at Poplar depot on 31 August 2013. **Antony Guppy**

3.3. EDINBURGH TRAMS

Network: 8.5 miles. **Lines:** 1. **Depots:** 1 (Gogar). **First opened:** 2014.
www.edinburghtrams.com **System:** 750 V DC overhead.

The newest tramway in the UK is situated in Edinburgh, the capital of Scotland with a population of around 500000. It finally opened on 31 May 2014, after several years of delays. The current 8½ mile route is around half of what had been planned to be built, hence the large fleet of 27 trams. The whole project, managed by the since disbanded Transport Initiatives Edinburgh (TIE) was dogged by delays, escalating costs, construction problems and contractual disputes. This saw the scheme, on which construction started in 2008, significantly scaled back to an Edinburgh city centre–Edinburgh Airport tramway, serving the suburbs of Balgreen and Saughton and the business parks around Edinburgh Gateway and Edinburgh Park. A tram stop is also provided for the Murrayfield rugby stadium.

While in the suburbs the tramway is mainly segregated, in the city centre there is street running via Haymarket station, Princes Street and St Andrews Square to the terminus at York Place, close to the city's bus station. Unfortunately there is not a stop ideally placed for Waverley station, passengers being advised to use the St Andrews Square stop and walk down the hill.

It is still hoped to extend the tramway in the future, and the tram fleet is large enough to support this. The original plan had been to run eastwards from Edinburgh city centre to the Port of Leith, Newhaven and then return to Haymarket via a loop via Granton and Roseburn.

The tramway is operated by Edinburgh Trams Ltd, a publicly owned company that works in partnership with Lothian Buses, as part of the Transport for Edinburgh Group.

A fleet of 27 7-section articulated CAF Urbos cars mounted on four bogies were ordered for the tramway. The trams are of a similar design to those used on the Midland Metro. At 42 m these are the longest trams to operate in the UK and the interior specification is high, with leather seats and large luggage racks for airport passengers. All trams offer free wi-fi. As well as the 78 seats there is room for 170 standing passengers. All trams were delivered in 2011–12, well ahead of the opening of the tramway. The tram numbers follow on the sequence used for the old Edinburgh tramway, which closed in 1956. The livery is similar to that used on Lothian buses – white, burgundy and grey, with black window surrounds.

Services operate from around 05.30 to midnight, although the last departure from the Airport is much earlier than that at 22.45. All services operate the full length of the line during the day, although some early morning and late evening trams terminate at Gyle Centre before running to or from the depot. Daytime frequency was improved at the start of 2017, and trams now operate approximately every 7 minutes, with an end-to-end journey time of 37 minutes. Three additional trams are used at peak times, including three extra services both in the morning and evening peaks introduced in July 2016 as a result of heavy peak-time demand.

The off-peak service all week therefore requires 12 trams in traffic from the fleet of 27. The diagramming for the peak hours is complex, and the working timetable shows three extra trams used at peak times. This nominally means that 15 trams should be seen in service during a whole weekday, but such is the size of the fleet that different trams may appear on the evening peak diagrams compared to those used in the mornings.

The depot and control centre are located at Gogar, near the Gogarburn stop, and given the large tram fleet a number of vehicles can normally be seen stabled in the yard. There are connections on both sides of the depot, so trams can leave empty for the short run to the Airport or to Gyle Centre to start in traffic. In terms of observing the trams, anywhere on the route should see all those in traffic, although Princes Street – Edinburgh's main shopping street – is an interesting place to watch trams mingling with buses, including special buses offering tours of the city. The Transport for Edinburgh mobile phone app should also be mentioned: as well as live running information this gives details of which trams are in traffic at any given time.

Tickets must be purchased before boarding the tram from one of the ticket machines located on the tram stop platforms. Single tickets start from £1.60, with a day ticket valid on trams and Lothian buses costing £4 for the City zone (all trams apart from Ingliston–Airport), or £9 for the Airport zone, covering all of the tram route. The excessive £5 additional charge for ¾ mile of track between Ingliston and the Airport has been criticised by many, especially when Airlink buses complete the same journey from the centre of Edinburgh for a cheaper fare than the trams.

EDINBURGH TRAMS

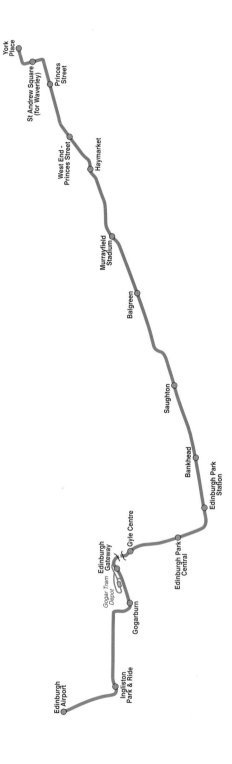

York
Place

St Andrew Square
(for Waverley)

Princes
Street

West End -
Princes Street

Haymarket

Murrayfield
Stadium

Balgreen

Saughton

Bankhead

Edinburgh Park
Station

Gyle Centre

Edinburgh
Gateway

*Gogar Tram
Depot*

Edinburgh Park
Central

Gogarburn

Ingliston
Park & Ride

Edinburgh
Airport

Passenger numbers to date have been encouraging, and in 2016 there were 5.6 million passenger journeys, a year-on-year growth of 10%. The city council supports a future extension of the tramway to Newhaven via Leith Walk, although this is not a view shared by the current Scottish Government.

CAF URBOS 3   7-SECTION TRAMS

Built: 2009–11 by CAF, Irun, Spain.
Wheel Arrangement: Bo-Bo-2-Bo.
Seats: 78.
Dimensions: 42.80 x 2.65 m.
Couplers: Albert.
Doors: Sliding plug.

Traction Motors: 12 x CAF of 80 kW (107 hp).
Weight: 56.25 tonnes.
Braking: Regenerative & electro hydraulic.
Maximum Speed: 50 mph.

251	257	263	268	273
252	258	264	269	274
253	259	265	270	275
254	260	266	271	276
255	261	267	272	277
256	262			

▲ Between Saughton and Edinburgh Park the tramway runs parallel with the Edinburgh–Glasgow main railway line, on this section the tramway reuses the former West Edinburgh busway as a trackbed. On 10 September 2014 264 is seen near the Bankhead stop. **Robert Pritchard**

▲ On the ¾-mile stretch of line between Ingliston Park & Ride and Edinburgh Airport (for which a premium fare must be paid), the tramway runs through open country. On 18 October 2014 260 has just left the Airport with an afternoon service for York Place. **Robert Pritchard**

▼ 275 passes Waverley Station as it heads onto Princes Street with a service for the Airport on 18 October 2014. **Robert Pritchard**

▲ 277 climbs to the point where the tramway crosses the Edinburgh–Glasgow main railway line near Saughton on its way to the Airport on 10 September 2014. Edinburgh Castle can be seen on the skyline. **Robert Pritchard**

3.4. GLASGOW SUBWAY

Network: 6.5 miles. **Lines:** 1 (Circular). **Depots:** 1 (Broomloan). **First opened:** 1896.
www.spt.co.uk/subway **System:** 600 V DC third rail.

This circular 4ft (1219mm) gauge underground line is the smallest metro system in the UK, running for 6½ miles underneath Glasgow city centre and the city's west end. Although not the capital, Glasgow is Scotland's largest city, with a population of around 600000. Owned and operated by Strathclyde Partnership for Transport the system has 15 stations, eight of which are to the north of the River Clyde and seven to the south. The steepest gradient is 1 in 20, between Govan and Partick. The entire passenger railway is underground, contained in twin-bore tunnels, allowing for clockwise operation on the "Outer" circle and anti-clockwise operation on the "Inner" circle. There are crossovers between the Inner and Outer circles between Govan and Ibrox stations.

The system is the world's third oldest underground railway after London and Budapest, and celebrated its 120th anniversary in December 2016. When opened it was the world's only cable-operated underground railway, driven by a stationary steam boiler. It changed to electric operation in 1935 using a 600 V DC third rail system. Even after electrification the original wooden-bodied vehicles were still used, being converted to electric units. They remained in traffic for some 80 years, with the Subway closing for major modernisation of the stations, tracks and rolling stock in May 1977. A number of the older cars are preserved and these are listed here.

Metro-Cammell was awarded the contract to build 33 new single power cars, which would normally operate in pairs as 2-car units. They used GEC traction motors. In 1992 these were joined by eight intermediate trailer cars, whose bodyshells were constructed at Hunslet TPL in Leeds. Final assembly took place at Hunslet Barclay, Kilmarnock. This brought the fleet size to 41 vehicles, allowing 3-car operation. All seating is longitudinal.

On reopening in April 1980 the system was nicknamed the "Clockwork Orange", inspired by the orange livery carried by the trains. The current, third, livery carried by the existing rolling stock is orange, grey and white and was introduced in 2011. Various cars have carried advertising liveries at different times.

Today all trains are formed of 3-cars: this is either two power cars sandwiching one of the trailer cars or three power cars. Trains run in semi-automatic mode in passenger service, meaning that speed and stopping are controlled by an Automatic Train Operation (ATO) system.

It takes 24 minutes to complete the loop in either direction. Trains run every 4 minutes at peak times, so 12 trains are needed for the peak service – this means 36 of the available 41 vehicles are required. Outer Circle peak trains run as Turns 1–6 and Inner Circle peak trains run as Turns 11–16. At off-peak times during the day trains run every 6 minutes, and then every 8 minutes after 19.00 and on Sundays (the system only operates between 10.00 and 18.00 on Sundays).

Both the depot and Subway control centre are at Broomloan, near Govan. At the time of the Subway modernisation in the late 1970s, access tracks to the depot were built: previously trains had to be lifted from the main tracks onto the depot tracks using a crane. Today all trains return to the depot overnight. The depot access tracks and the depot itself are the only part of the system that is above ground. The depot complex includes a test track, mainly used for driver training or testing trains after maintenance. Also based here are four 4-wheel battery electric locomotives used for permanent way work, although L2 and L3 are not in use at the time of writing.

In 2016 it was announced that Stadler had won the tender to supply the next generation of trains for the Subway, as part of a £288 million upgrade, with Italian company Ansaldo responsible for resignalling the system. There will be 17 new 4-car driverless trains, which will feature through gangways and a new forward view for passengers to enjoy. The two centre cars will be shorter, and articulated. Each train will be 39.2 m long, slightly longer than the existing 3-car sets. TSA of Austria will supply the traction motors for the new trains. The first new rolling stock is expected to be delivered in 2019, entering service in 2020, initially manually driven using a temporary cab. From 2021 it is planned to introduce "Unattended Train Operation" (UTO) with no driver. Resignalling will enable the current 4-minute headway to be reduced to just 1½ minutes.

Comprehensive refurbishment of each of the stations started in 2011 and will continue over the coming years. In addition all 28 of the system's escalators have been replaced. While SPT considers it impracticable to make all Subway stations wheelchair accessible, lifts will be provided at St Enoch (the closest station to Glasgow Central) and Govan. As part of the upgrade for new rolling stock half-height platform edge screen doors will be installed at stations.

GLASGOW SUBWAY

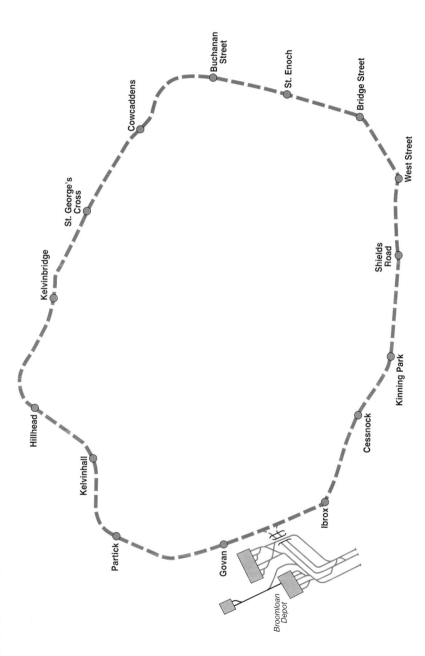

Buchanan Street

Cowcaddens

St. Enoch

St. George's Cross

Bridge Street

Kelvinbridge

West Street

Hillhead

Shields Road

Kelvinhall

Kinning Park

Partick

Cessnock

Govan

Ibrox

Broomloan Depot

All stations are staffed and have ticket gates which check your ticket on entry. Tickets can be purchased from staff or from ticket machines. A single ticket costs £1.60 in 2017, and an all-day ticket is £4. For £6.80 the good-value Glasgow Roundabout Ticket includes the Subway and also suburban rail services around Glasgow.

Various expansion plans have been discussed over the years but none have been progressed further so the network today is the same as it was when it opened in 1896. 12.7 million passengers were carried on the Subway in 2015–16.

DRIVING POWER CARS

Built: 1977–79 by Metro-Cammell, Birmingham. Refurbished 1993–95 by ABB Derby.
Wheel Arrangement: Bo-Bo.   **Traction Motors:** 4 x GEC G312AZ of 35.6 kW (48 hp).
Seats: 36.   **Weight:** 19.6 tonnes.
Dimensions: 12.81 m x 2.34 m.   **Braking:** Disc.
Couplers: Wedgelock.   **Maximum Speed:** 33.5 mph.
Doors: Sliding.
Non-Standard Liveries: 101 – Original Glasgow Subway (maroon & cream).
                   130 – Possible future Subway livery (white & orange).

101	**0**	108		115		122		128	
102		109		116		123		129	
103		110		117		124		130	**0**
104		111		118		125		131	
105		112		119		126		132	
106		113		120		127		133	
107		114		121					

INTERMEDIATE BOGIE TRAILERS

Built: 1992 by Hunslet TPL, Leeds/Hunslet Barclay, Kilmarnock.
Wheel Arrangement: 2-2.   **Traction Motors:** –
Seats: 40.   **Weight:** 17.2 tonnes.
Dimensions: 12.70 m x 2.34 m.   **Braking:** Disc.
Couplers: Wedgelock.   **Maximum Speed:** 33.5 mph.
Doors: Sliding.

201	203	205	207	208
202	204	206		

BATTERY ELECTRIC WORKS LOCOMOTIVES

Built: 1977 by Clayton Equipment, Hatton.
Battery: Battery pack of 94 lead acid cells (188V).   **Wheel Arrangement:** Bo.
Traction Motors: 2 x GEC G312AZ of 35.6 kW (48 hp) series wound.
Dimensions: 4.70 m x 2.10 m.   **Couplers:** Wedgelock.
Weight: 14.8 tonnes.   **Maximum Speed:** 15 mph.

L2	LOBEY DOSSER		L3	RANK BAJIN

BATTERY ELECTRIC WORKS LOCOMOTIVES

Built: 2010 by Clayton Equipment, Hatton.
Battery: Battery pack of 100 lead acid cells (200V).   **Wheel Arrangement:** Bo.
Traction Motors: 2 x 56 kW (75hp) series wound.
Dimensions: 6.61 m x 2.10 m.   **Couplers:** Wedgelock.
Weight: 15 tonnes.   **Maximum Speed:** 15 mph.

L6	L7

▲ Repainted into original Subway livery to mark the 120th anniversary is car 101, which also now carries No.55. On 14 December 2016, the date of the 120th anniversary, 101+201+130 arrive at West Street, one of the stations with a narrow island platform, with an Outer Circle service.

Robin Ralston

▼ 108+128+114 arrive at the refurbished Govan station with an Inner Circle service on 28 November 2016.

Robin Ralston

▲ 119+205+132 arrive at Hillhead with a Sunday morning Outer Circle service on 14 December 2014. **Robert Pritchard**

▼ Intermediate trailer car 204 at Govan on 28 November 2016. **Robin Ralston**

3.4.1. GLASGOW SUBWAY PRESERVED STOCK

A number of the original Glasgow Subway vehicles have been preserved, and these are listed below.

GLASGOW DISTRICT SUBWAY COMPANY CARS

Built: 1896–1901 by Oldbury Railway Carriage & Wagon Company, Oldbury as Gripper cars, converted to motor cars 1935, or 1897–98 by Hurst Nelson & Company, Motherwell as Trailer cars.

Gripper	12.42 x	m	tons	42 seats.
Trailer	7.62* x	m	tons	24 seats. * Later extended to 12 m.

1	Gripper	Glasgow Museum Resources Centre, Nitshill	Oldbury 1896
4†	Gripper	Glasgow Riverside Museum	Oldbury 1896
7	Gripper	Brooklands Pleasure Park, Lancing	Oldbury 1896
39	Trailer	Glasgow Riverside Museum	Hurst Nelson 1898
41†	Trailer	Glasgow Museum Resources Centre, Nitshill	Hurst Nelson 1898
55	Gripper	Bo'ness & Kinneil Railway	Oldbury 1901

† Only part of the original vehicles survives.

▲ Original Glasgow Subway Gripper car 55 is preserved in the Scottish Railway Preservation Society's museum at Bo'ness, where it is seen on 23 July 2016. **Robert Pritchard**

3.5. GREATER MANCHESTER METROLINK

Network: 59 miles. **Lines:** 8. **Depots:** 2 (Queens Road and Trafford). **First opened:** 1992.
www.metrolink.co.uk
System: 750 V DC overhead.

Metrolink was the first modern tramway system in the UK when it opened in 1992, combining street running in the city centre with longer distance running over former BR lines. Conversion of the Bury–Victoria line to a tramway and the replacement of obsolete EMUs on this route was first proposed as part of a 1982 study, which suggested a six-route light rail system. When the system opened it had 26 trams and operated from Bury to Altrincham with a street section through the centre of Manchester and a spur to Piccadilly station (crucially linking Victoria and Piccadilly stations). Since then, in comparison with most of the other UK tramways, Metrolink has expanded considerably, the number of extensions opening in the last 6 years being particularly extraordinary, and testament to the dedication of Greater Manchester PTE (now Transport for Greater Manchester (TfGM)) and its faith in the continued growth of the Metrolink system.

Manchester is a city of just over 500 000 population, although the Metropolitan area of Greater Manchester also includes many other large towns, such as Bury, Salford, Oldham, Rochdale, Stockport and Bolton, some places now served by the Metrolink network.

Metrolink is owned by Transport for Greater Manchester, the transport delivery arm for the Greater Manchester Combined Authority which is made up of the ten Greater Manchester councils. TfGM is responsible for investment in Metrolink and its transport services and facilities, but sub-contracts the day-to-day operation of the tramway. At the time of writing Metrolink is operated by RATP Dev (the French company that also runs the Paris Metro). RATP Dev started operating Metrolink in 2011, when it acquired Stagecoach Metrolink (which had been awarded a 10-year contract to operate Metrolink in 2007). A new operator will take over in July 2017, with KeolisAmey (the same partnership that operates Docklands Light Railway in London) having been awarded a 10-year contract to operate Metrolink until 2027. The new operator plans to recruit 300 more staff and to increase the staff presence on the network.

After the initial Bury/Altrincham–Piccadilly route, the first extension was a line from Cornbrook to Eccles which opened in 1999–2000. This route features quite a lot of street-running. After a gap of 10 years the next round of extensions followed in quick succession, almost tripling the length of the system in 5 years. First was a short spur off the Eccles line to MediaCityUK, which opened in September 2010. The first part of the South Manchester Line to Chorlton and St Werburgh's Road opened in summer 2011 and this was further extended (along the former Manchester South District Railway and Midland Railway line) to East Didsbury in 2013.

It had long been an aspiration to convert the Oldham loop to a tramway, to provide a more frequent service and take people into the centre of Manchester. The national rail Oldham loop line closed for rebuilding in October 2009, reopening from Manchester to Oldham Mumps in summer 2012. The original alignment here only lasted a year and a half, being replaced by a new alignment through Oldham town centre which opened at the start of 2014. Meanwhile the top end of the loop line to Rochdale reopened as a tramway in late 2012/early 2013. A further extension into Rochdale town centre followed in spring 2014.

East of Piccadilly the East Manchester Line reached Droylsden in February 2013 and this was followed by Droylsden–Ashton-under-Lyne in October 2013, on a route that features some longer sections of street running. In late 2014 St Werburgh's Road–Manchester Airport opened, offering a mix of segregated and street running and connecting the communities of Baguley and Wythenshawe. The final new line was the Second City Crossing. This was a short but important section of track in the city centre – the original city crossing via Mosley Street was by now getting very congested and in order to cross more trams from one side of the city to the other a second route was needed. The route chosen was from St Peter's Square, which was rebuilt with four platforms, along Cross Street to Exchange Square and then to Victoria. The first part of the Second City Crossing, known locally as "2CC" from Victoria to Exchange Square, opened in late 2015 and then the remainder to St Peter's Square in February 2017. 2CC is initially being used by trams from East Didsbury to Rochdale or Shaw & Crompton.

The opening dates of the various lines are as summarised below:

6 April 1992: Bury–Victoria.
27 April 1992: Victoria–Deansgate-Castlefield.
15 June 1992: Deansgate–Altrincham.

GREATER MANCHESTER
METROLINK

Rochdale Town Centre
Newbold
Rochdale Railway Station
Kingsway Business Park
Milnrow
Newhey
Shaw and Crompton
Derker
Oldham Central
Westwood
Oldham Mumps
Freehold
Oldham King Street
Oldham Moss
South Chadderton
Hollinwood
Failsworth
Newton Heath and Moston
Central Park
Monsall
Bury
Radcliffe
Whitefield
Whitefield Tunnel
Besses o' th' Barn
Bury Old Road Tunnel
Prestwich
Heaton Park Tunnel
Heaton Park
Bowker Vale
Crumpsall
Abraham Moss
Rochdale Road Tunnel
Queens Road
Queens Road Depot
Ashton West
Ashton-under-Lyne
Ashton Moss
Victoria
Collyhurst Tunnel
Etihad Campus
Clayton Hall
Cemetery Road
Exchange Square
Holt Town
New Islington
Velopark
Edge Lane
Droylsden
Audenshaw
Eccles
Ladywell
Weaste
Langworthy
Broadway
Harbour City
Anchorage
Salford Quays
Exchange Quay
Pomona
Cornbrook
Deansgate-Castlefield
Piccadilly
MediaCityUK
Trafford Centre
Parkway
Village
Imperial War Museum
Wharfside
Approved Extension
EventCity
a - Shudehill
b - Market Street
c - Piccadilly Gardens
d - St Peter's Square
Old Trafford
Trafford Bar
Trafford Depot
Firswood
Stretford
Chorlton
St Werburgh's Road
Withington
Sale Water Park
Barlow Moor Road
Burton Road
Dane Road
West Didsbury
Sale
Brooklands
Northern Moor
Didsbury Village
East Didsbury
Timperley
Wythenshawe Park
Moor Road
Baguley
Navigation Road
Martinscroft
Roundthorn
Altrincham
Benchill
Crossacres
Wythenshawe Town Centre
Robinswood Road
Peel Hall
Manchester Airport
Shadowmoss

20 July 1992: Market Street–Piccadilly.
6 December 1999: Cornbrook–Broadway.
21 July 2000: Broadway–Eccles.
20 September 2010: Harbour City–MediaCityUK.
7 July 2011: Trafford Bar–St Werburgh's Road.
13 June 2012: Victoria–Oldham Mumps.
16 December 2012: Oldham Mumps–Shaw & Crompton.
8 February 2013: Piccadilly–Droylsden.
28 February 2013: Shaw & Crompton–Rochdale Railway Station.
23 May 2013: St Werburgh's Road–East Didsbury.
9 October 2013: Droylsden–Ashton-under-Lyne.
27 January 2014: Freehold–Derker via Oldham Central.
31 March 2014: Rochdale Railway Station–Rochdale Town Centre.
3 November 2014: St Werburgh's Road–Manchester Airport.
6 December 2015: Victoria–Exchange Square.
26 February 2017: Exchange Square–St Peters Square (Second City Crossing).

It was decided at an early stage that Manchester would be a high-floor network, because of the existing high platforms on the Bury and Altrincham lines inherited from BR. Therefore on the street running sections, high-floor platforms were constructed.

Despite now having 93 stops, almost 60 miles of track, eight different routes, and two different routes across Manchester city centre, Metrolink doesn't use route numbers, letters or colours on its trams – only on the route map where letters (and different colours to indicate the routes) are used. All routes run to a 12 minute frequency at both peak and off-peak times on Mondays–Saturdays (until around 20.00). This gives a service every 6 minutes on large parts of the system – for example on the original lines to Bury and Altrincham and to Harbour City, St Werburgh's Road and Shaw & Crompton. The route letters used on the map and the journey time of the different routes are as follows:

A: Altrincham–Market Street–Bury: journey time 55 minutes;
B: Altrincham–Piccadilly–Etihad Campus: journey time 37 minutes;
C: Bury–Piccadilly: journey time 36 minutes;
D: MediaCityUK–Piccadilly: journey time 22 minutes;
E: Eccles–Piccadilly–Ashton-under-Lyne: journey time 60 minutes;
F: Manchester Airport–Deansgate–Castlefield*: journey time 44 minutes;
G: East Didsbury–Exchange Square–Rochdale Town Centre: journey time 1h16;
H: East Didsbury–Shaw & Crompton: journey time 1h01.
*   To be extended to Victoria via Exchange Square later in 2017.

Most routes operate from around 05.30 to midnight. In 2016 very early morning services were introduced on the Airport route, specifically aimed at airport workers or those passengers with early flights. The first service runs empty from Trafford depot to Firswood where it leaves at 03.06, arriving at the Airport at 03.43. Trams then run every 20 minutes from Deansgate-Castlefield until 06.00, when the normal 12-minute frequency starts. On weekdays all services on route A (Altrincham–Bury) are pairs of trams, as are some on routes G and H from East Didsbury. Additional trams operate in connection with football matches at Old Trafford (Manchester United) or the Etihad Stadium (Manchester City).

On Sundays lines A, D and H do not run and line D to Eccles runs via MediaCityUK. The other five routes operate to the standard 12-minute frequency on Sundays.

The original fleet consisted of 26 articulated two-section T68 trams supplied by Firema of Italy, which were numbered 1001–1026. These were supplemented by six similar vehicles (2001–2006), built in 1999 for the Eccles extension. By 2007 more trams were needed, initially to alleviate overcrowding and also to serve planned new extensions. The "Flexity Swift" M5000 model from Bombardier was selected, closely based on the K5000 high-floor cars supplied for the Cologne Stadtbahn light rail system in Germany. The M5000s offered a similar capacity to a T68, although with around 30 fewer seats, but 146 standing spaces. The first M5000 (numbered 3001) arrived in July 2009 and entered traffic in December of that year.

The last T68s were withdrawn from normal service in April 2014. The majority were scrapped but 1003 found further use with the Greater Manchester Fire Service for training purposes and four of the class were moved to Long Marston for UKTram. A further four are still stored at Metrolink depots, two of which are reserved for the Heaton Park Tramway.

The M5000s were ordered in a number of different batches between 2007 and 2014, the fleet of 120 cars being delivered between 2009 and 2016. The first 12 were ordered in 2007 – eight to

▲ 3033 arrives at Newhey on the Oldham loop line, which was converted from a railway line into a tramway, on 25 May 2013. **Robert Pritchard**

▼ 3046 leaves Victoria station, heading into the city centre, with an Altrincham service on 8 October 2016. **Robert Pritchard**

alleviate overcrowding on the existing system and four for the new MediaCityUK extension. This was followed in June 2008 by an order for another 28 for the extensions to Oldham/Rochdale and St Werburgh's Road. Another eight were ordered in March 2010 for the East Didsbury and Ashton extensions, and this was followed by another 14 in July 2010 for the Airport line and the Oldham and Rochdale town centre lines.

As thoughts turned to replacement of the by now ageing and unreliable T68s (it was established that the M5000s were four times more reliable than the T68s), 12 more M5000s were ordered in September 2011 to replace the 12 T68s in the worst condition. In July 2012 there was an order for another 20 M5000s after the decision was taken to withdraw all the T68s. In January 2014 ten more were ordered for the forthcoming Trafford Park extension (although not due to open until 2020) and this was followed by an order for 12 in July 2014 and a final four in September 2014, both to enable more double trams to operate. Metrolink has options with Bombardier for up to another 21 cars, should they be required.

The M5000s were assembled at the Bombardier plant in Vienna, but the sub-assemblies and primary parts are manufactured in Bautzen, Germany, with the underframes coming from Česká Lípa in the Czech Republic and electrical equipment supplied by Vossloh Kiepe. The M5000s are double-ended articulated trams with three bogies, the two outer bogies being powered. From car 3075 upwards the seating layout was modified, with eight more seats (60 instead of 52). Metrolink is the only UK tram network that uses pairs of trams in normal service (the M5000s and before them the T68s both operate as double trams on certain routes).

Although outwardly the same, the M5000s are operationally split into two fleets: 3001–3060 are fitted with Automatic Tram Stop (ATS) and Vehicle Recognition System (VRS) and can be used on all routes. 3061–3120 are not fitted with these systems and are only used on the routes to Rochdale, Manchester Airport, East Didsbury and Ashton-under-Lyne.

When first opened with T68s the Metrolink livery was white, grey and blue. When the M5000s were delivered the livery was changed to silver and yellow.

The M5000s are maintained at both depots. The original depot and workshops is located at Queens Road, adjacent to the Bury line. A second depot opened in 2010 to maintain the growing fleet, this is located at Trafford, close to Old Trafford station.

Since the opening of the Second City Crossing, the busiest stop on the network is Deansgate-Castlefield, which has 30 trams timetabled to pass through every hour in each direction, plus the services terminating from Manchester Airport (that will be extended to Victoria). All except route C (Bury–Piccadilly) can be seen here. The Piccadilly Gardens triangle is also a good place to observe the trams, and all except the Manchester Airport trams and the two routes taking the Second City Crossing can be seen here.

Tickets must be purchased from the ticket machines at stops before boarding the tram. Single and return tickets are available, with a city centre zone single costing £1.20. A Peak Day Travelcard valid on trams only is £7, an Off-Peak Travelcard costing £5 and one for a weekend (valid after 18.00 Fridays) costing £5.80. There are various other tickets available also covering buses and trains within Greater Manchester, and also the GM Wayfarer, which for £12 allows off-peak travel on trains, trams and buses throughout Greater Manchester and also parts of Cheshire, Derbyshire, Lancashire, Staffordshire and the Peak District.

Not surprisingly, considering it is by far the largest tramway network in the UK, Metrolink in 2015–16 carried 34.3 million passengers according to DfT figures, an increase of 10% on the previous year and more than Birmingham, Blackpool, Nottingham and Sheffield combined. In the 2016 calendar year Metrolink figures showed that the system carried 37 million passengers. According to DfT figures the Metrolink vehicle miles in 2015–16 were 7.2 million miles, an increase of 27% on the previous year.

Work started in 2017 on a 3½ mile extension from Pomona to Trafford Centre, which will have five intermediate stops and is planned to open in late 2020. It is planned that trams from Trafford Centre will operate to Crumpsall via the Second City Crossing. In the future TfGM is watching developments with the South Yorkshire tram-train scheme closely, with a view to possibly having something similar in Manchester, in particular for the Manchester–Bredbury–Marple route. Another proposal is for a loop line around Wythenshawe (on the Airport route), to better serve Wythenshawe hospital.

T68 1000 SERIES
2-SECTION TRAMS

Built: 1991–92 by Firema, Italy. Chopper control.
Wheel Arrangement: Bo-2-Bo.   **Traction Motors:** 4 x GEC of 130 kW (174 hp).
Seats: 82 (+4).   **Weight:** 45 tonnes.
Dimensions: 29.00 x 2.65 m.   **Braking:** Regenerative, disc & emergency track.
Couplers: Scharfenberg.   **Maximum Speed:** 50 mph.
Doors: Sliding.
Livery: White, dark grey & blue with light blue doors.

1007, 1020 and 1023 are stored at Trafford depot.
1016, 1022, 1024 and 1026 are stored at Long Marston for use in UK Tram development work.

1007	(S)	EAST LANCASHIRE RAILWAY	1023	(S)	
1016	(S)		1024	(S)	
1020	(S)		1026	(S)	
1022	(S)				

T68 2000 SERIES
2-SECTION TRAMS

Built: 1999 by Ansaldo, Italy. Chopper control.
Wheel Arrangement: Bo-2-Bo.   **Traction Motors:** 4 x GEC of 130 kW (174 hp).
Seats: 82 (+4).   **Weight:** 45 tonnes.
Dimensions: 29.00 x 2.65 m.   **Braking:** Regenerative, disc & magnetic track.
Couplers: Scharfenberg.   **Maximum Speed:** 50 mph.
Doors: Sliding.
Livery: White, dark grey & blue with light blue doors.

2001 is stored at Trafford depot.

2001   (S)

▲ 3002 arrives at the then new Rochdale Station stop, with the St John the Baptist RC Church as an impressive backdrop, with a service from East Didsbury on 25 May 2013.   **Robert Pritchard**

▲ On 29 November 2016 3050+3054 wait in the Sheffield Street turnback siding, just beyond Piccadilly station, waiting to head back towards the city centre with an Altrincham service.
Robert Pritchard

▼ 3063 crosses the River Mersey between the Barlow Moor and Sale Water Park stops with a Cornbrook–Manchester Airport service on 31 October 2016. **Robert Pritchard**

3000 SERIES   FLEXITY SWIFT   2-SECTION TRAMS

Built: 2009–16 by Bombardier, Vienna, Austria.
Wheel Arrangement: Bo-2-Bo.
Traction Motors: 4 x Vossloh Kiepe 3-phase asynchronous of 120 kW (161 hp).
Seats: 52 (3001–3074) or 60 (3075–3120).   **Weight:** 39.7 tonnes.
Dimensions: 28.40 x 2.65 m.   **Braking:** Regenerative, disc & magnetic track.
Couplers: Scharfenberg.   **Maximum Speed:** 50 mph.
Doors: Sliding.
Livery: Silver & yellow.
Advertising Livery: 3095 – Key 103 (pink & black)

3004, 3005, 3014, 3016, 3017, 3021, 3032 3051 and 3055 have been fitted with "ice-breaking" pantographs.

3001	3025	3049	3073	3097
3002	3026	3050	3074	3098
3003	3027	3051	3075	3099
3004	3028	3052	3076	3100
3005	3029	3053	3077	3101
3006	3030	3054	3078	3102
3007	3031	3055	3079	3103
3008	3032	3056	3080	3104
3009	3033	3057	3081	3105
3010	3034	3058	3082	3106
3011	3035	3059	3083	3107
3012	3036	3060	3084	3108
3013	3037	3061	3085	3109
3014	3038	3062	3086	3110
3015	3039	3063	3087	3111
3016	3040	3064	3088	3112
3017	3041	3065	3089	3113
3018	3042	3066	3090	3114
3019	3043	3067	3091	3115
3020	3044	3068	3092	3116
3021	3045	3069	3093	3117
3022	3046	3070	3094	3118
3023	3047	3071	3095 **AL**	3119
3024	3048	3072	3096	3120

Names:

3009   50th Anniversary of Coronation Street 1960–2010
3020   LANCASHIRE FUSILIER
3098   Gracie Fields

SPECIAL PURPOSE VEHICLE

Purpose-built 4-wheel diesel-hydraulic multi-purpose locomotive (with crane) for shunting, engineering or tram recovery work. Normally based at Queens Road depot.

Built: 1991 by RFS Industries, Kilnhurst.
Engine: Caterpillar 3306 PCT of 170 kW.   **Wheel Arrangement:** Bo.
Transmission: Hydraulic. Rockwell T280.
Dimensions: 8.20 x 2.50 m.   **Couplers:** Scharfenberg.
Weight: 22 tonnes.   **Maximum Speed:** 25 mph.

1027

3.6. LONDON TRAMLINK

Network: 17.5 miles. **Lines:** 4. **Depots:** 1 (Therapia Lane). **First opened:** 2000.
www.tfl.gov.uk/trams **System:** 750 V DC overhead.

The London Tramlink system, initially called "Croydon Tramlink", runs through central Croydon (one of the southern Greater London boroughs) via a one-way loop, with lines radiating out to Wimbledon, New Addington, Beckenham Junction and Elmers End. The system opened on 10 May 2000, returning trams to the streets of London for the first time in almost 50 years (the New Addington branch opened first, followed by the other lines later in May 2000). Tramlink is operated by Tram Operations Ltd, a subsidiary of the major train and bus operator First Group, on behalf of Transport for London.

Tramlink grew out of a transport study carried out by London Transport and BR in 1986 covering all of Greater London, plus a need to provide better rail or tram services in the area and link previously separate routes. While most of the network serves areas which already had rail connections, New Addington had never before had any kind of rail service, and this is served by a mostly new alignment purpose-built for trams, plus part of the former Elmers End–Sanderstead rail route (closed 1983), including the 500 m tunnel just beyond Sandilands. Unlike most other UK street-running tramways, little of the on-street sections shares road space with private cars.

Much of the rest of the system uses former railway lines: the Wimbledon line and part of the eastern route which covers most of the old Elmers End–Addiscombe branch. Both the Wimbledon and Addiscombe branches closed in 1997 to allow for conversion to the tramway. These are combined with some street running through a large central Croydon city loop, which is used by trams from Elmers End and Beckenham Junction (Lines 1/2) in a clockwise direction. In the centre of Croydon eastbound trams on Lines 3 and 4 run via Tamworth Road, West Croydon station and Wellesley Road while westbound trams use George Street. The hub of the operation is East Croydon main line station, where all services can be seen. The four routes operate as follows, with the normal weekday daytime frequency given (the peak service is roughly the same as the off-peak service, with 22 trams an hour passing East Croydon in each direction):

Line 1: Elmers End–West Croydon (every 15 minutes);
Line 2: Beckenham Junction–West Croydon (every 10 minutes and every 15 minutes evenings);
Line 3: New Addington–East Croydon–Wimbledon every 7/8 minutes (every 15 minutes weekend evenings);
Line 4: Elmers End–East Croydon–Wimbledon (every 15 minutes, no Sunday service).

Line 4 was introduced in 2012 from Elmers End to Therapia Lane and was extended to Wimbledon in 2016 following the doubling of some of the single track sections and the delivery of more trams. The doubling gave capacity for 12 trams an hour on the Wimbledon branch, although services finish on Line 4 at 19.00. A second platform was also built at the Wimbledon terminus in 2015 to increase operating flexibility.

Both the Tramlink depot and control centre are located at Therapia Lane, which is on the Wimbledon line. Tramlink operates for close to 22 hours a day, in terms of the last trams arriving at the depot and the first leaving the next morning. Compared to some other systems early morning and late evening positioning trips operate as normal services, rather than empty stock. The working timetable shows the first departure from Therapia Lane at 04.16 to New Addington, with the last arrival back at Therapia Lane being at 01.41 (from Beckenham Junction). The longest journey on the network is on Line 3, which takes 46 minutes end-to-end.

When the system opened in 2000 it was operated by a fleet of 24 Bombardier 3-section "Flexity Swift" six-axle CR4000 trams, closely based on the K4000 trams built for the Cologne low-floor network in Germany. These are mostly low-floor, although there is a short high-floor section at the outer end over the motor bogies. The unusual number series (2530 onwards) carries on from where the old London tram fleet left off.

Although there have been no extensions to the original system, passenger growth has been such that a new fleet of trams was required. The first of six Stadler Variobahn trams (the first three of these had been built ahead of schedule for Bergen, Norway but were diverted to Croydon), which are 5-section, fully low-floor trams and slightly longer than the original trams, entered traffic in spring 2012. Smaller orders for another four (2560–63) which arrived in 2015 and a final two (2564–65) which arrived in 2016 followed. Initially used on the new Line 4, the 12 Stadler trams are now used across the whole system alongside the original fleet.

LONDON TRAMLINK

All trams always operate singly. The current timetable requires 30 trams in operation from the fleet of 36 (although this includes the out-of-traffic 2551): Three trams on Line 1, six on Line 2, 14 on Line 3 and seven on Line 4.

On 9 November 2016 London Tramlink suffered a serious accident, when tram 2551 overturned on the tight curve at Sandilands, the tram having taken the curve at more than three times the permitted speed. Seven people lost their lives in the accident, which is the worst in modern UK tramway history. Tram 2551 is now stored at an RAIB site at Farnborough, and such was the damage caused when the tram overturned that it may be beyond economic repair.

The original livery was red and white, based on that of the old London trams. In 2008 this was changed to light grey and lime green, with a blue solebar, the lime green colour being used to denote Tramlink on the TfL zonal Travelcard map. Various advertisement or promotional liveries have been carried by some trams at different times.

London Tramlink forms an integral part of the TfL network, with interchange available at several places to heavy rail or LUL (at Wimbledon). The whole of the network is within Travelcard Zone 4. A single fare with an Oystercard smartcard is £1.50, with a single paper ticket being £2.60. Tickets must be purchased from ticket machines at the stops before boarding the tram. A Zones 1–4 or 1–6 Travelcard is valid on all tram services, as is a One Day Bus & Tram Pass (at the time of writing £5).

27 million passengers used Tramlink in 2015–16, although this was a decline of 12% compared to the previous year as a result of closures for track relaying in the centre of Croydon. However, Tramlink is still the second busiest UK tramway (as opposed to a Metro) network after Manchester Metrolink. Plans for extensions to Crystal Palace and Sutton have been proposed in recent years but the only new track currently planned is the Dingwall Road loop, a new turning loop close to East Croydon station. The current single track city centre loop has limited capacity and some of the trams running from the three eastern branches (particularly from New Addington) into central Croydon would be able to use the new loop to turn, allowing more services on the eastern branches. This is planned for completion in autumn 2019. A second platform and double tracking at Elmers End is also planned.

BOMBARDIER FLEXITY SWIFT — 3-SECTION TRAMS

Built: 1998–99 by Bombardier, Vienna, Austria.
Wheel Arrangement: Bo-2-Bo.
Seats: 70.
Dimensions: 30.10 x 2.65 m.
Couplers: Scharfenberg.
Doors: Sliding plug.
Advertising Livery: 2537 – Turkish Airlines.

Traction Motors: 4 x 120 kW (161 hp).
Weight: 36.3 tonnes.
Braking: Disc, regenerative and magnetic track.
Maximum Speed: 50 mph.

2530	2535	2540	2545	2550
2531	2536	2541	2546	2551 (S)
2532	2537 **AL**	2542	2547	2552
2533	2538	2543	2548	2553
2534	2539	2544	2549	

Name:

2535   STEPHEN PARASCANDOLO 1980–2007

STADLER VARIOBAHN — 5-SECTION TRAMS

Built: 2011–16 by Stadler, Berlin, Germany.
Wheel Arrangement: Bo-2-Bo.
Seats: 74.
Dimensions: 32.40 x 2.65 m.
Couplers: Albert.
Doors: Sliding plug.
Advertising Livery: 2554 – Love Croydon (purple & blue).

Traction Motors: 8 x 45 kW (60 hp).
Weight: 41.5 tonnes.
Braking: Disc, regenerative and magnetic track.
Maximum Speed: 50 mph.

2554 **AL**	2557	2560	2562	2564
2555	2558	2561	2563	2565
2556	2559			

▲ Bombardier Flexity Swift 2539 is seen near Addiscombe with a Line 1 service from Elmers End to West Croydon on 5 October 2014. **Brian Denton**

▼ 2553 leaves East Croydon with a Line 3 service from New Addington to Wimbledon on 15 October 2016. **Robert Pritchard**

▲ Two Stadler cars cross at Dundonald Road on 11 April 2015. 2557 leaves with a Line 3 Wimbledon–Reeves Corner service as 2558 arrives with a service for Wimbledon (Tramlink through Croydon town centre was closed on this day for engineering works). **Robert Pritchard**

▼ 2558 arrives at Mitcham Junction on 11 April 2015 with a Wimbledon–Reeves Corner Line 3 service. **Robert Pritchard**

3.7. MIDLAND METRO

Network: 13 miles.   **Lines:** 1.   **Depots:** 1 (Wednesbury).   **First opened:** 1999.
www.nxbus.co.uk/the-metro   **System:** 750 V DC overhead.

Birmingham is the UK's second biggest city with a population of around 1.1 million. The Midland Metro tramway opened on 31 May 1999 with a 12-mile line between Birmingham's Snow Hill station and Wolverhampton, along the former Great Western Railway line via Handsworth, West Bromwich and Wednesbury (the GWR line terminated at Wolverhampton Low Level, with passenger services withdrawn in 1972 and freight in 1992). The old railway route has been rebuilt with new low floor platform stations. Approaching Wolverhampton Midland Metro leaves the old railway alignment, with around 1½ miles of street-running to the St Georges terminus, close to the main shopping area in the town (but not so convenient for the railway station).

A short but significant extension opened in 2015–16 when the tramway was extended through Birmingham city centre, first to Bull Street and then to a new terminus outside the recently redeveloped New Street station, called "Grand Central" after the adjacent shopping centre. This extension resulted in the original cramped Snow Hill terminus being abandoned as trams now use a new alignment to join street level near Bull Street.

The tramway is owned by the West Midlands Combined Authority (WMCA), and is operated by National Express Midland Metro (formerly Travel Midland Metro).

The Monday–Saturday off-peak service frequency is every 8 minutes, increasing to every 6 minutes at peak times on weekdays. During the evening and on Sundays trams operate every 15 minutes. There are some short workings to and from Wednesbury Parkway for trams booked to run on or off the depot at peak times, but otherwise all trips operate the length of the route – the end-to-end journey time is 40 minutes across the 26 stops. 15 trams are required at peak times, with 12 trams needed to maintain the off-peak service. Trams operate from around 05.00 to midnight.

For the first 15–16 years of operation the tramway used 16 2-section Ansaldo T69 trams built in Italy. However, these were not popular and were unreliable, some spending lengthy periods out of traffic or being used for spares to keep other members of the class in traffic. As part of the upgrading of the tramway and the New Street extension, in 2012 20 new CAF trams were ordered, this was later increased to 21. The new CAF trams were delivered between October 2013 and July 2015, the first officially entering service in September 2014. The last of the T69s were withdrawn in August 2015. All of the older trams are now stored at the Long Marston site in Warwickshire, apart from No. 16 which is still at Wednesbury depot. Officially the trams have been retained for "future projects", such as the new Wednesbury–Brierley Hill extension, but whether they see use again remains to be seen.

The new vehicles are 5-section articulated bi-directional trams built by CAF in Spain. They provide the same number of seats as the older trams, but are longer so with more room for standees. They are also 100% low floor. As well as the 52 seats there is quoted to be capacity for 156 standing passengers. At the same time as the new trams were delivered the depot at Wednesbury was extended to make it long enough to hold two of the longer trams.

The livery used for the original trams was blue and red, but a new pink, silver and white scheme was introduced in 2007 (although it was only applied to four of the older trams). A revised version of this new livery was applied to the new CAF trams.

Further extensions are planned and are being managed by the Midland Metro Alliance, a consortium that will "implement a 10-year programme of tram system enhancement works". The first extension will be a short link from the current terminus at Grand Central to Centenary Square via Victoria Square, with construction beginning in 2017 and opening planned in late 2019. Uniquely, for this section of line trams are planned to operate on battery power throughout, and all of the CAF trams will be modified to operate as such (the first, 18, was returned to Spain for modification in January 2017). The rest of the fleet will be modified at Wednesbury depot. Lithium ion batteries will be fitted to the trams' roofs and will be recharged by the overhead line along other parts of the route. The Midland Metro will be the first commercial tram system in the UK to have catenary-free running, allowing trams to operate over short distances without the need for overhead wires, which it is said would have marred the architecturally sensitive area around Birmingham's historic town hall in Victoria Square.

Wolverhampton Station
Approved Extension
Wolverhampton St Georges
The Royal
Priestfield
The Crescent
Bilston Central
Loxdale
Bradley Lane
Wednesbury Parkway
Wednesbury Depot
Wednesbury, Great Western Street
Swan Village Hill Top Tunnel
Black Lake
Dudley Street Guns Village
Dartmouth Street
Lodge Road West Bromwich Town Hall
West Bromwich Central
Trinity Way
Kenrick Park
The Hawthorns
Handsworth Booth Street
Winson Green Outer Circle
Soho Benson Road
Jewellery Quarter
Hockley Tunnels
St. Paul's
St. Chads
Bull Street
Corporation Street
Grand Central
Proposed Victoria Extension Square
Centenary Square

MIDLAND METRO

At the other end of the route a short half-mile extension is planned through Wolverhampton city centre to terminate at the railway station. This is also planned to open in 2019. Trams will then serve both St Georges and the railway station in Wolverhampton. The next extension will run for around 1 mile from Centenary Square to Brindleyplace, Five Ways and Edgbaston, planned to open in spring 2021. This will be followed (in 2022–23) by the 1-mile Birmingham Eastside extension. This will leave the Birmingham city centre route between Bull Street and Corporation Street and run to Digbeth High Street and High Street Deritend, including a stop at Curzon Street station (the planned new HS2 station for Birmingham). All of these routes will also feature some catenary-free running.

Meanwhile in early 2017 vegetation clearance started with a view to opening a 7½ mile link south from Wednesbury to Dudley Port, Dudley and the Merry Hill shopping centre at Brierley Hill. This runs largely along the former South Staffordshire Railway alignment, with some street running in Dudley town centre. It is hoped to open this line in 2023. There are also at an early stage for a 10-mile extension from Digbeth to Heartlands Hospital, the NEC/Birmingham Airport and the HS2 Interchange Station in north Solihull, with the hope that this will open in 2026.

The Centenary Square/Edgbaston and Wolverhampton extensions can be serviced by the existing fleet of 21 trams (although this will mean a peak requirement of 19 trams). Further trams (and a second depot) will be needed for the Eastside/Airport and Brierley Hill extensions.

Tickets range from just £1 for a short city centre hop to £5 for a Metro+bus off-peak Daysave ticket. Midland Metro is also included in the West Midlands Daytripper ticket (£6.60). In terms of observing the trams, all services can be seen in Birmingham city centre, and the Wednesbury stops can also be interesting in terms of viewing trams running on and off the depot.

According to the DfT 2015–16 figures Midland Metro carried the fewest passengers of any of the UK tramways – 4.8 million (slightly fewer than Blackpool, but up almost 11% on the previous year). However, the extension into Birmingham city centre should see this increase for the year 2016–17 and Midland Metro figures released as this book closed for press showed that 6.6 million passengers used Metro during the calendar year of 2016.

▲ On 5 September 2014, the day the new CAF trams entered traffic, car 23 pauses at The Hawthorns with a service for Birmingham Snow Hill.   **Robert Pritchard**

ANSALDO T69   3-SECTION TRAMS

Built: 1998–99 by Ansaldo Transporti, Italy.
Wheel Arrangement: Bo-2-Bo.
Seats: 52.
Dimensions: 24.00 x 2.65 m.
Couplers: Not equipped.
Doors: Sliding plug.

Traction Motors: 4 x 105 kW (140 hp).
Weight: 35.6 tonnes.
Braking: Regenerative, disc and magnetic track.
Maximum Speed: 43 mph.

Standard livery: Dark blue & light grey with a green stripe & red front end.
Other/Non-Standard Liveries: **MW:** Network West Midlands silver & pink.
                                  0: Original Birmingham Corporation tram livery (cream & blue).

All stored at Long Marston except 16 at Wednesbury depot.

01 (S)	05 (S) **MW**	08 (S)	11 (S) **0**	14 (S)
02 (S)	06 (S)	09 (S) **MW**	12 (S)	15 (S)
03 (S)	07 (S) **MW**	10 (S) **MW**	13 (S)	16 (S)
04 (S)				

CAF URBOS 3   5-SECTION TRAMS

Built: 2013–14 by CAF, Zaragoza, Spain.
Wheel Arrangement: Bo-2-Bo.
Seats: 52.
Dimensions: 32.96 x 2.65 m.
Couplers: Albert.
Doors: Sliding plug.

Traction Motors: 8 x 65 kW (87 hp).
Weight: 41.0 tonnes.
Braking: Regenerative, disc and magnetic track.
Maximum Speed: 43 mph.

Livery: Network West Midlands silver & pink.

17	22	26	30	34
18	23	27	31	35
19	24	28	32	36
20	25	29	33	37
21				

Names:

35	Angus Adams		37	OZZY OSBOURNE

▲ Clearly showing that this was once a main line railway, 23 is seen again leaving Black Lake for Snow Hill on 5 September 2014. **Robert Pritchard**

▼ 29 approaches the Wolverhampton St Georges terminus with a service from Snow Hill on 10 June 2015. **Cliff Beeton**

▲ 33 leaves the Corporation Street stop in Birmingham city centre with a service for Wolverhampton on 10 December 2016. **Robert Pritchard**

▼ Running on a short section of grass track on the Birmingham city centre extension between Bull Street and St Chads on 11 June 2016 is 37 with a service for Wolverhampton. St Chads was originally named Snow Hill, but was later changed as it is actually better to alight at Bull Street for Snow Hill station. **Robert Pritchard**

3.8. NOTTINGHAM EXPRESS TRANSIT

Network: 20 miles.   **Lines:** 2.   **Depots:** 1 (Wilkinson Street).   **First opened:** 2004.
www.thetram.net   **System:** 750 V DC overhead.

Nottingham is a city of around 320000. The Nottingham Express Transit light rail system was first conceived in 1988 as a joint venture between Nottingham City Council and Nottinghamshire County Council. Approved in 1998, it opened on 9 March 2004, with a line from Station Street running for around 8 miles north to Hucknall, plus a 1 mile spur to Phoenix Park, where there is a large Park & Ride car park. The first part of this route involves around 3 miles of street running in Nottingham, including through old Market Square and a bi-directional single track section through the Hyson Green area. The northern part of the route runs mainly parallel with the Nottingham–Mansfield–Worksop railway line. North of Bulwell both the tramway and railway line are single track, with crossing loops at stops for the tramway. At the northern terminus at Hucknall there is a railway/tramway interchange station.

On 25 August 2015 the system doubled in length, from around 10 to 20 miles with the opening of two extensions south and west from Station Street. At the same time the Station Street stop was itself moved onto a new viaduct which now carries trams over Nottingham station. The two new lines diverge almost immediately south of the station, one route running to Clifton South via Wilford and the other to Toton Lane (Chilwell) via Beeston. Both routes feature long sections of on-street running and part of the Clifton South branch follows the alignment of the old Great Central line from Nottingham Victoria towards Loughborough. The Toton Lane line serves the large ng2 business park, Queen's Medical Centre and Nottingham University, as well as the residential districts of Beeston and Chilwell.

Although NET refers to the system as three Lines (Line 1 to Hucknall/Phoenix Park, Line 2 to Clifton South and Line 3 to Toton Lane), this has no relevance to the service pattern. Trams run on two (unnumbered) routes, the longest being Hucknall–Toton Lane, which takes 63 minutes and the other being Phoenix Park–Clifton South which takes 46 minutes. The new extended system has 51 stops.

Nottingham Express Transit was originally operated by a joint consortium of Nottingham City Council and Transdev, but since 2011 has been operated by the Tramlink Nottingham consortium (formed of Alstom Transport, Keolis, Wellglade, Meridiam Infrastructure, InfraVia and VINCI Construction UK).

Trams operate from around 06.00 to midnight. The weekday off-peak services is every 10 minutes on both routes, this gives a 5-minute frequency on the Wilkinson Street–Nottingham city centre–Nottingham Station section of the route. 32 trams out of the overall fleet of 37 are required for daily service on weekdays. Off peak the Hucknall–Toton Lane service requires 15 trams, plus three additional at peak times. The Phoenix Park–Clifton South route requires ten trams off-peak, and an additional four at peak times. The additional peak-hour trams provide a frequency of every 3–4 minutes between Wilkinson Street and Nottingham Station and of approximately every 8 minutes on the rest of each route.

The original fleet consisted of 15 Bombardier built Incentro AT6/5 trams (built to an Adtranz design). These were supplemented by 22 new Alstom Citadis 302 trams, of a similar design to those built for Dublin. These were delivered between September 2013 and August 2014 for the new extensions. Both the Incentro and Citadis trams are bi-directional, 100% low-floor trams with five articulated sections riding on two motor bogies (at the outer ends) and one trailer bogie. In the Citadis trams, as well as the 58 seats (plus ten tip-ups) there is space for 144 standing passengers. The Incentro trams have space for 129 standing passengers.

The first of the new Alstom trams entered service in July 2014 on the existing system. As both types of tram have a similar seating and standing capacity they are used interchangeably across both routes.

Livery is an attractive silver and dark green, with black window surrounds. NET has named all its trams after personalities or famous sportsmen or women from the local area.

The depot and workshop at Wilkinson Street was built with the capacity for a large fleet – when the new Alstom trams arrived some additional stabling sidings were added. There are connections from the depot for trams to both head north (towards Hucknall) or south (towards the city). Alstom is contracted to maintain both the original Bombardier trams and its own Citadis trams.

▲ One of the original Bombardier cars, 201 "Torvill and Dean", arrives at the Old Market Square stop in the centre of Nottingham with a service for Station Street on 3 August 2014. **Robert Pritchard**

▼ Carrying a lime green livery, 209 "Sidney Standard" passes The Exchange shopping centre having just left Old Market Square stop with a Hucknall–Toton Lane service on 17 July 2016. **Robert Pritchard**

A single ticket between any two stops on the network is £2.20. A day ticket offering unlimited travel is £4. Nottingham trams originally used conductors on all trams who sold tickets, but when the 2015 extensions opened this was changed to a system of roving ticket inspectors. Now all tickets must be purchased before boarding the tram.

In terms of observing the trams, the Nottingham Station stop is good, with all services passing through. Old Market Square stop in the city centre is also good, although it can be tricky for photographs. Wilkinson Street stop outside the depot has the added interest of trams running on and off the depot before and after the morning/evening peaks.

As can be expected passenger numbers have increased significantly since the new extensions opened in August 2015. The 2015–16 passenger figures show 12.2 million passengers used NET, an increase of 50% on the previous year – and the extensions were not open for all of this period.

A number of other extensions have been talked about, in particular extending the Toton Lane line to terminate at the planned new High Speed 2 parkway station at Toton. A feasibility study is in place into a possible 3-mile extension from Phoenix Park to Kimberley. More ambitious proposals have included a tramway linking Nottingham and Derby.

BOMBARDIER INCENTRO   5-SECTION TRAMS

Built: 2002–03 by Bombardier, Derby Litchurch Lane Works.
Wheel Arrangement: Bo-2-Bo.   **Traction Motors:** 8 x 45 kW (65 hp) wheelmotors.
Seats: 54 (+4).   **Weight:** 36.7 tonnes.
Dimensions: 33.00 x 2.40 m.   **Doors:** Sliding plug.
Braking: Disc, regenerative and magnetic track for emergency use.
Couplers: Not equipped.   **Maximum Speed:** 50 mph.
Non-Standard/Advertising Liveries: 206 – jet2.com (red & blue).
                       207 – purple & white.
                       209 – lime green.
                       211 – Deliveroo (green, purple & blue).

201		Torvill and Dean	209	**0**	Sydney Standard
202		DH Lawrence	210		Sir Jesse Boot
203		Bendigo Thompson	211	**AL**	Robin Hood
204		Erica Beardsmore	212		William Booth
205		Lord Byron	213		Mary Potter
206	**AL**	Angela Alcock	214		Dennis McCarthy MBE
207	**0**	Mavis Worthington	215		Brian Clough
208		Dinah Minton			

ALSTOM CITADIS 302   5-SECTION TRAMS

Built: 2013–14 by Alstom, Barcelona, Spain.
Wheel Arrangement: Bo-2-Bo.   **Traction Motors:** 4 x 120 kW (161 hp).
Seats: 58 (+10).   **Weight:** 40.8 tonnes.
Dimensions: 32.00 x 2.40 m.   **Doors:** Sliding plug.
Braking: Disc, regenerative and magnetic track for emergency use.
Couplers: Not equipped.   **Maximum Speed:** 50 mph.

216	Dame Laura Knight	227	Sir Peter Mansfield
217	Carl Froch MBE	228	Local Armed Forces Heroes
218	Jim Taylor	229	Viv Anderson MBE
219	Alan Sillitoe	230	George Green
220	Aprille Jones	231	Rebecca Adlington OBE
221	Stephen Lowe	232	William Ivory
222	Michelle and Richard Daniels	233	Ada Lovelace
223	Colin Slater MBE	234	George Africanus
224	Vicky McClure	235	David Clarke
225	Doug Scott CBE	236	Sat Bains
226	Jimmy Sirrel & Jack Wheeler	237	Stuart Broad MBE

NOTTINGHAM EXPRESS TRANSIT

▲ Alstom Citadis tram 218 approaches the Phoenix Park terminus with a service from Station Street on 3 August 2014. **Robert Pritchard**

▼ 223 "Barbara White OBE" passes Beeston Parish Church, between the Beeston Centre and Chilwell Road stops, with a Hucknall–Toton Lane service on 17 July 2016. **Robert Pritchard**

3.9. SOUTH YORKSHIRE SUPERTRAM

Network: 18 miles.   **Lines:** 3.   **Depots:** 1 (Nunnery).   **First opened:** 1994.
www.supertram.com   **System:** 750 V DC overhead.

Sheffield is a city of around 500000. The South Yorkshire Supertram system opened in stages during 1994 and 1995, having been first conceived during feasibility studies in the 1980s, with tramway construction beginning in 1991. The network has three lines radiating from Sheffield city centre. These run to Halfway in the south-east with a spur from Gleadless Townend to Herdings Park, to Middlewood in the north with a spur from Hillsborough to Malin Bridge and to Meadowhall Interchange in the north-east, adjacent to the large shopping complex. Opening dates in 1994–95 were as follows:

21 March 1994: Fitzalan Square–Meadowhall;
22 August 1994: Fitzalan Square–Spring Lane;
5 December 1994: Spring Lane–Gleadless Townend;
17–18 February 1995: Fitzalan Square–Shalesmoor;
27 March 1995: Gleadless Townend–Halfway;
3 April 1995: Gleadless Townend–Herdings Park;
23 October 1995: Shalesmoor–Middlewood/Malin Bridge.

Supertram was the first low-floor tram system in Britain when in opened in 1994, two years after the high-floor Manchester system. Unlike some other tramways it does not use any former railway lines, with a mix of on-street and segregated running (54% of track is embedded or street-running rail). The Meadowhall branch is mostly segregated with longer sections of the Hillsborough and Halfway routes having street running. There are 48 stops on the system.

The system was originally operated by South Yorkshire Supertram Ltd (SYSL), a subsidiary of South Yorkshire Passenger Transport Executive (SYPTE). SYSL was sold to bus and train operator Stagecoach in 1997, and this company has operated the trams since then, branded as "Stagecoach Supertram". Stagecoach is also responsible for the maintenance of the fleet at the Nunnery depot, which is adjacent to the Nunnery Square stop. Stagecoach has an agreement to operate Supertram until 2024.

The fleet of 25 trams were obtained from Siemens-Duewag in Germany, and are widely recognised as the most comfortable trams in the UK. The cars are owned by South Yorkshire Light Rail Ltd, a subsidiary of SYPTE. They are all-steel, double-ended in three articulated sections with eight powered axles: because of severe gradients on the hills in Sheffield (up to 1 in 10) all axles are powered. The outer sections are low floor (with a high-floor seating section immediately behind each cab) and the centre section, on which the pantograph is located, is high floor. As well as the 86 seats the trams can take 162 standing passengers.

Four of the trams are not in their original A+B+C formation following accidents. Trams 02 and 11 (as they were then numbered) were damaged in separate accidents in 1995. 02 returned to traffic as two sections of 02 and one of 11 and 11 with two sections of 11 and one of 02. In 2015 cars 118 and 120 collided with each other and one section of 118 was formed with two from 120 to return "120" to traffic. All four trams 102, 111, 118 and 120 remain permanently misformed.

There have been no significant changes to the system, either in terms of route or service changes, or new vehicles since it opened in 1994–95. However, in 2012 the Department for Transport chose Sheffield as the pilot for a tram-train project, which would see tram-trains used on both the existing network and on a new route to Rotherham. Originally due to be completed by 2016 delays to the track works have put the expected start date for the tram-train scheme back to summer 2018. The tram-train to Rotherham will operate for a minimum of 5 years, with the first 2 years being the pilot period, fully funded by the DfT. It will be jointly operated by Supertram and Arriva Northern.

The first of the seven new tram-trains, built by Vossloh (now Stadler) in Spain was delivered in late 2015, with the remainder following in 2016. The first of these vehicles were due to be introduced on the existing system in spring 2017. When tram-train starts it is planned that four vehicles will be dedicated to the Cathedral–Rotherham route (three cars in traffic on a 20 minute service) and the other three on existing routes. The tram-trains are branded as Vossloh Citylink cars, and are similar to the original trams, being 3-section with a high-floor centre section (without doors). They also have four bogies, but only three are powered. They have been built as dual-voltage, in case the line through Rotherham should be converted to the standard railway 25 kV AC system in the future. For operation on Network Rail lines EMU unit

SOUTH YORKSHIRE SUPERTRAM

Sheffield Tram - Train Extension
(under construction)

Continued from above

Continued from above

Continued Below

Parkgate

Rotherham Central

Meadowhall South / Tinsley

Meadowhall Interchange

Carbrook

Valley Centertainment

Arena / Don Valley

Attercliffe

Woodbourn Road

Cricket Inn Road

Nunnery Depot

Nunnery Square

Hyde Park

Sheffield Station / Sheffield Hallam University

Cathedral

Fitzalan Square

Castle Square

City Hall

West Street

Granville Road / The Sheffield College

Park Grange Croft

Park Grange

Spring Lane

Arbourthorne Road

Manor Top / Elm Tree

Hollinsend

White Lane

Hackenthorpe

Donetsk Way

Crystal Peaks

Moss Way

Birley Moor Road

Birley Lane

Gleadless Townend

Herdings / Leighton Road

Herdings Park

Beighton / Drake House Lane

Waterthorpe

Westfield

Halfway

Infirmary Road

Langsett / Primrose View

Shalesmoor

Netherthorpe Road

University of Sheffield

Hillsborough

Bamforth Street

Malin Bridge

Hillsborough Park

Leppings Lane

Middlewood

numbers 399 201–207 are carried (as well as vehicle numbers in the 999xxx series). Supertram fleet numbers are 201–207. These vehicles are also fitted with safety equipment for operating on the national railway network, such as TPWS and OTMR.

The tram-trains will leave the existing system via a new chord near the Meadowhall South/ Tinsley stop, joining the current freight only line from there to Rotherham Central, and then terminating around 1½ miles further north outside the Rotherham Parkgate retail complex.

On the existing system, before the tram-train operation starts, there are three routes, colour coded as Yellow, Blue and Purple. These colours are displayed on the front of trams. The normal weekday daytime schedule is as follows:

Yellow: Middlewood–Cathedral–Meadowhall; Every 10 minutes, journey time 34–38 minutes;
Blue: Malin Bridge–Cathedral–Halfway; Every 10 minutes, journey time 41–44 minutes;
Purple: Herdings Park–Cathedral–Meadowhall. Every 30 minutes, journey time 40 minutes*.
*   Mon–Fri daytime only, operates every 20 minutes Cathedral–Herdings Park at peak times.

Trams operate between around 06.00 and midnight. Additional peak-hour trips operate on the Yellow and Blue routes. At evenings and on Sundays all three routes operate a 20-minute service meaning that the short Herdings Park branch actually has a better service then, as both the Blue and Purple routes run every 20 minutes, giving a 10 minute core service on the city centre–Gleadless Townend section, and every 20 minutes to Halfway and Herdings Park.

22 trams are required for the peak service, with 21 at off-peak times. All routes operate on the Cathedral–Fitzalan Square section in the city centre, meaning this is the best place for observing trams. The Cathedral stop can be regarded as the hub of the operation and has the added interest of Purple route trams reversing. The busy Hillsborough–city centre route also has a tram every 5 minutes as it is covered by both the Yellow and Blue routes. A number of early morning and late evening services use the north side of the Park Square triangle when they are running from the depot to form early morning services or returning to the depot at night. These services can be worked out from the timetable as they are those that start or terminate at Cricket Inn Road and then next call at Sheffield Station.

▲ Carrying an advertising livery for East Midlands Trains, 111 leaves the Cathedral stop with a Yellow route service from Middlewood to Meadowhall on 19 August 2015.   **Robert Pritchard**

▲ 112 is seen between the Westfield and Waterthorpe stops on the Halfway line, with a Blue route service to Malin Bridge on 15 May 2010. **Robert Pritchard**

▼ During a public open day at the Nunnery depot on 25 October 2015 cars 124 and 115 receive maintenance. **Robert Pritchard**

The trams have carried three different liveries, being delivered in a plain grey livery, this was replaced by a mainly white Stagecoach livery (when the trams were renumbered from 01–25 to 101–125) and then the present standard Stagecoach blue, red and orange livery, which was first introduced in 2006. Various advertisement liveries have also been carried, and in 2010 tram 120 received a version of the original Sheffield Corporation tram livery of cream and blue to mark 50 years since the closure of the original Sheffield tramway in 1960.

Tickets are purchased on board the tram from the conductor. A single ticket costs from £1.70, with an all day Supertram ticket costing £4, or one for Stagecoach buses and trams in Sheffield costing £4.20. A Sheffield Citywide at £4.60 covers all trams and buses in Sheffield, while a South Yorkshire Connect+ day ticket at £7.90 gives unlimited travel on buses, trams and trains in South Yorkshire.

Sheffield Supertram was used by 11.6 million passengers in 2015–16, a figure that has dropped from the 15 million mark between 2007 and 2012 through a combination of disruption caused by line closures for track relaying works and more competitive ticket pricing by bus operators. Sheffield has the highest percentage of journeys by concessionaries in the country (29%). Other than tram-train to Rotherham there are no extensions to the system currently planned.

SIEMENS   3-SECTION TRAMS

Built: 1993–94 by Siemens-Duewag, Düsseldorf, Germany.
Wheel Arrangement: B-B-B-B.
Traction Motors: 4 x monomotor drives of 265 kW (355 hp).
Seats: 80 (+6).   **Weight:** 52 tonnes.
Dimensions: 34.75 x 2.65 m.   **Braking:** Regenerative, disc & emergency track.
Couplers: Albert (emergency use).   **Maximum Speed:** 50 mph.
Doors: Sliding plug.
Non-Standard/Advertising Liveries: 111 and 116 – East Midlands Trains (blue).
                                      120 – Original Sheffield Corporation (cream & blue).

101	106	111 **AL**	116 **AL**	121
102	107	112	117	122
103	108	113	118	123
104	109	114	119	124
105	110	115	120 **0**	125

VOSSLOH/STADLER CITYLINK   3-SECTION TRAM-TRAINS

Built: 2015–16 by Vossloh/Stadler, Valencia, Spain.
Systems: 750 V DC/25 kV AC overhead.
Wheel Arrangement: Bo-2-Bo-Bo.   **Traction Motors:** 6 x VEM of 145 kW (195 hp).
Seats: 88 (+8).   **Weight:** 64 tonnes.
Dimensions: 37.20 x 2.65 m.   **Braking:** Regenerative, disc & emergency track.
Couplers: Albert (emergency use).   **Maximum Speed:** 60 mph.
Doors: Sliding plug.

For operation on Network Rail EMU numbers 399 201–207 are also carried.

201	203	205	206	207
202	204			

▲ 119 approaches the Hillsborough stop with a Yellow route service from Meadowhall to Middlewood on 16 August 2016. **Robert Pritchard**

▼ New Vossloh Citylink tram-train 399 204 stands at the Halfway terminus on 30 January 2017. The tram had been on test during the night but had failed and was repaired here during the day.
Paul Beardsley

3.10. TYNE & WEAR METRO

Network: 48 miles.   **Lines:** 2.   **Depots:** 1 (South Gosforth).   **First opened:** 1980.
www.nexus.org.uk/metro   **System:** 1500 V DC overhead.

The impressive and efficient Tyne & Wear Metro system covers 48 route miles and can be described as the UK's first modern light rail system. The initial network opened between 1980 and 1984, consisting of a line from South Shields via Gateshead and Newcastle Central to Bank Foot (later extended to Newcastle Airport in 1991) and the North Tyneside loop (over former BR lines) serving Tynemouth and Whitley Bay with a terminus in the city centre at St James. A more recent extension was from Pelaw to Sunderland and South Hylton in 2002, using existing heavy rail infrastructure between Heworth and Sunderland. Opening dates for the various sections were as follows:

11 August 1980: Haymarket–South Gosforth–Whitley Bay–Tynemouth;
10 May 1981: South Gosforth–Bank Foot;
15 November 1981: Haymarket–Heworth;
14 November 1982: St James–Monument–North Shields–Tynemouth;
24 March 1984: Heworth–Pelaw–South Shields;
17 November 1991: Bank Foot–Newcastle Airport;
31 March 2002: Pelaw–Sunderland–South Hylton.

More stations were slowly added in following years to give today's total of 60 stations. The most recent was Simonside, opened in March 2008.

The network runs over a mixture of former heavy rail lines and in newly constructed tunnels under central Newcastle (two new viaducts were also needed). There are nine stations that are fully underground. Sunderland is the only station where heavy rail and Metro trains share the same platforms.

Operationally there are two routes, coloured Green and Yellow on the official route maps. The Green route runs from the Airport, to the North-West of Newcastle, through the city to Gateshead and out to Sunderland and South Hylton in the south. The journey time for this route is scheduled to take between 1h04 and 1h07 minutes.

The Yellow route is more complex, operating as a loop and branch. Starting from St James in the city centre trains head east to North Shields and then anti-clockwise around the Coast loop via Whitley Bay, through Newcastle and south-east to South Shields. On arrival at South Shields a train will then complete this route in reverse, ie running to Newcastle, clockwise around the Coast loop via Whitley Bay and North Shields to St James. The journey time for a full Yellow route train is scheduled at 1h24.

The off-peak Monday–Friday and Saturday daytime service sees trains operate every 12 minutes on the full length of both routes, giving a service every 6 minutes on the core section between South Gosforth and Pelaw. At peak times additional services operate on the Yellow route every 12 minutes between Monkseaton, South Gosforth and Pelaw and on the Green route every 12 minutes between Regent Centre and Pelaw, giving a service every 3 minutes in both directions on the core section. Evening services operate every 15 minutes after around 19.00. On Sundays trains start running half-hourly and then from late morning operate every 15 minutes on both routes. The first trains on weekdays start running from 05.00 and finish at around 00.30.

The Metro system uses a fleet of 90 articulated twin Metro cars built by Metro-Cammell in Birmingham in the late 1970s to early 1980s, modelled on the German Stadtbahnwagen design. Of the three bogies, the outer two bogies are powered. Originally fitted with 84 seats, on mid-life refurbishment in the late 1990s/early 2000s the number of seats was reduced to 68 to allow for more standing space, with longitudinal instead of facing seating either side of the articulation. During a further major refurbishment between 2010 and 2015 at Wabtec Doncaster this was reduced to 64 seats to incorporate two dedicated wheelchair spaces. The crush loading capacity is quoted at 232 passengers per car.

There are half-width driving cabs at each end, with seats opposite them – giving passengers the unusual opportunity to sit "alongside the driver" and have a view of the line ahead. Because enough trains were originally built to allow 3-train operation – which was never implemented – there were enough trains in the fleet to cover both the Airport and South Hylton extensions.

Funding constraints meant that the latest fleet refurbishment only included 86 cars – 4001/02/40/83 were not refurbished and officially now form a reserve fleet, although do still see

▲ 4045+4019 cross the River Wear on the impressive 1879 Monkwearmouth viaduct, between St Peter's and Sunderland stations, with an Airport–South Hylton service on 13 August 2016. **Robert Pritchard**

TYNE & WEAR METRO

Airport
Callerton Parkway
Bank Foot
Kingston Park
Fawdon
Wansbeck Road
Regent Centre
Palmersville
Northumberland Park
Shiremoor
West Monkseaton
Monkseaton
Whitley Bay
Cullercoats
Tynemouth
North Shields
North Shields Tunnel
Meadow Well
Percy Main
Howdon
Hadrian Road
Wallsend
Benton
Four Lane Ends
Longbenton
South Gosforth
Gosforth Depot
Ilford Road
West Jesmond
Jesmond
Walkergate
Chillingham Road
Byker
Byker Tunnel
Haymarket
St James
Monument
Manors
Newcastle Central
Gateshead
Gateshead Stadium
Felling
Pelaw
Heworth
Fellgate
Brockley Whins
Simonside
Bede
Hebburn
Jarrow
Tyne Dock
Tyne Dock Tunnel
Chichester
South Shields
East Boldon
Seaburn
Stadium of Light
St Peter's
Sunderland
Park Lane
University
Millfield
Pallion
South Hylton

regular use. Apart from five units in advertising liveries, and 4001 in its 1975 style original livery, the rest of the fleet now carries a smart metallic silver, black and yellow livery, which can look very different depending on the lighting conditions.

Metro cars always operate in pairs (in the early years of the Metro cars operated singly on midweek evenings and winter Sundays). The Monday–Friday off-peak service requires 27 pairs (54 cars in traffic), 15 pairs on the Yellow route and 12 pairs on the Green route. An additional 12 pairs are used in the morning peak (nine Yellow/three Green) and 11 pairs in the evening peak (eight Yellow/three Green), this means that from the fleet of 90 cars, 78 are required in the morning peak and 76 in the evening peak. Extra trains run as required at weekends and evenings in connection with football matches at both St James Park (Newcastle) and the Stadium of Light (Sunderland).

Metro also owns three battery electric locomotives and two Plasser & Theurer tampers. The locomotives are used for autumn railhead cleaning trains, depot shunting, engineering trains and to rescue failed Metro cars.

The system is publicly owned by Nexus (the Tyne & Wear Passenger Transport Executive) – Nexus also took direct control of the operation of Metro from DB Regio in April 2017 (DB Regio having operated Metro since 2010). Nexus has recently started to consult on the future of the Metro, and is developing a bid with the Government for funding to replace the existing fleet, which is now approaching 40 years old and, according to Tyne & Wear Metro "has passed its intended design life". It is hoped to have a new fleet of trains in traffic by around 2025.

Ridership in 2015–16 was 40.3 million passengers, up 6% on the previous year. The Metro control centre and depot are both based at South Gosforth.

All Metro stations are unstaffed, with ticket machines. Some stations now have ticket gates. Single, return and all-day tickets are available. An all-day Metro ticket costs £5 at the time of writing. This ticket is also valid on the Shields ferry, linking North and South Shields. For observation purposes the busiest section of line is that between South Gosforth and Pelaw, which sees all trains. West Jesmond or South Gosforth are probably the best stations for an observation, and in around 1h45 all services can be seen here. Between West Jesmond and Jesmond an interconnecting line runs to Manors – this is retained for empty stock movements.

▲ 4050+4031 stand at the recently modernised station of Haymarket with a service for St James via the Coast on 13 August 2016. **Robert Pritchard**

METRO-CAMMELL   2-SECTION UNITS

Built: 1978–81 by Metropolitan Cammell, Birmingham (prototype cars 4001 and 4002 were built by Metropolitan Cammell in 1975 and rebuilt 1984–87 by Hunslet TPL, Leeds).

Wheel Arrangement: B-2-B. **Traction Motors:** 2 x Siemens of 187 kW (250 hp) each.
Seats: 64 (* 68). **Weight:** 39.0 tonnes.
Dimensions: 27.80 x 2.65 m. **Braking:** Air/electro magnetic emergency track.
Couplers: BSI. **Maximum Speed:** 50 mph.
Doors: Sliding plug.
Non-Standard and Advertising Liveries: 4001 – Original 1975 Tyne & Wear Metro livery of yellow & cream.
4002 – Tyne & Wear Metro (orange & black).
4033, 4040, 4082 and 4083 – Emirates Airlines (red).

4001	*	**0**	4019		4037		4055		4073
4002	*	**AL**	4020		4038		4056		4074
4003			4021		4039		4057		4075
4004			4022		4040	*	**AL**	4058	4076
4005			4023		4041		4059		4077
4006			4024		4042		4060		4078
4007			4025		4043		4061		4079
4008			4026		4044		4062		4080
4009			4027		4045		4063		4081
4010			4028		4046		4064		4082	**AL**
4011			4029		4047		4065		4083	*	**AL**
4012			4030		4048		4066		4084
4013			4031		4049		4067		4085
4014			4032		4050		4068		4086
4015			4033	**AL**	4051		4069		4087
4016			4034		4052		4070		4088
4017			4035		4053		4071		4089
4018			4036		4054		4072		4090

BATTERY ELECTRIC WORKS LOCOMOTIVES

Built: 1988–89 by Hunslet TPL, Leeds.
Battery: **Wheel Arrangement:**
Traction Motors: 2 x Hunslet-Greenbat T9-4P of 67 kW (90 hp).
Dimensions: 6.30 m x 2.60 m. **Couplers:** BSI.
Weight: 26.25 tonnes. **Maximum Speed:** 30 mph.

Registered for operation on the national railway network as 97901–97903.

BL1 | BL2 | BL3

ON-TRACK MACHINES

–	Plasser & Theurer 08-16M Unimatic Tamper	Built: 1989
MA60	Plasser & Theurer 08-275NX Switch & Crossing Tamper	Built: 2013

▲ 4057+4048 arrive at Millfield, on the South Hylton branch, with a service for the Airport on 13 August 2016.
Robert Pritchard

▼ Battery electric works locomotives BL2 and BL1 top-and-tail an autumn Railhead Treatment Train through West Jesmond on 13 October 2016.
Justin Cazenave

APPENDIX I. LIST OF LOCATIONS

The following is a list of locations to accompany Sections 2: Preserved Underground Stock and Section 3.4.1: Glasgow Subway Preserved Stock. Ordnance Survey grid references are given for each location.

§   denotes site not generally open to the public.

OS GRID REF

Alderney Railway, Mannez Quarry, Isle of Alderney, Channel Islands.	–
Alstom Train Services, Morden Depot, 179 London Road, Morden, Greater London. §	TQ 255680
Bo'ness & Kinneil Railway, Bo'ness Station, Union Street, Bo'ness, Falkirk.	NT 003817
Brooklands Pleasure Park, Lakeshire, Western Road, Lancing, West Sussex.	TQ 173073
Buckinghamshire Railway Centre, Quainton Road Station, Aylesbury, Buckinghamshire.	SP 736189
Coopers Lane Primary School, Pragnell Road, Grove Park, Greater London. §	TQ 405728
Cravens Heritage Trains, Epping Signal Box, Epping Station, Epping, Essex. §	TL 462016
Glasgow Museum Resources Centre, 200 Woodhead Road, Nitshill, Glasgow. §	NS 520601
Glasgow Riverside Museum, Pointhouse Quay, Yorkshill, Glasgow.	NS 557661
Great Ormond Street Hospital, Great Ormond Street, Greater London.	TQ 305821
Hardingham Station, Low Street, Hardingham, Norfolk.	TG 050055
London Transport Museum, Covent Garden, Greater London.	TQ 303809
London Transport Depot Museum, Gunnersby Lane, Acton, Greater London.	TQ 194799
London Underground, Acton Works, 130 Bollo Lane, Acton, Greater London. §	TQ 193798
London Underground, Hainault Depot, Thurlow Gardens, Ilford, Greater London. §	TQ 450920
London Underground, Northfields Depot, Northfield Avenue, Brentford, Gtr London. §	TQ 166789
London Underground, Ruislip Depot, West End Road, Ruislip, Greater London. §	TQ 094862
Mangapps Railway Museum, Southminster Road, Burnham-on-Crouch, Essex.	TQ 944980
Nene Valley Railway, Wansford Station, Peterborough, Cambridgeshire.	TL 093979
Routemaster Heritage Centre, Units 90–95, Waterside Trading Estate, Trumpers Way, Hanwell, Greater London. §	TQ 153793
Sutton Hall Railway, Sutton Hall, Rochford, Essex.	TQ 888892
Tyne & Wear Fire Service Training Centre, Nissan Way, Barmston Meir, Washington, Tyne & Wear. §	NZ 329572
Village Underground, 54 Holwell Lane, off Bishopgate, Shoreditch, Greater London.	TQ 334823
Walthamstow Pumphouse Museum, The Pump House, Lowe Hall Lane, Walthamstow, Greater London.	TQ 362882
Westfield Storage, Westfield Park, Dinton, Wiltshire. §	SU 011312
Woodlands, Elm Hill, Coppleridge, Motcombe, near Shaftesbury, Dorset. §	ST 846267

APPENDIX II. ABBREVIATIONS USED

ATO	Automatic Train Operation
BR	British Railways, later British Rail
C&SL	City & South London Railway
CCE&H	Charing Cross, Euston & Hampstead Railway
CLRC	Central London Railway Company
DLR	Docklands Light Railway
DR	District Railway
EMU	Electric Multiple Unit
GNP&BR	Great Northern, Piccadilly & Brompton Railway
LER	London Electric Railways
LNER	London & North Eastern Railway
LPTB	London Passenger Transport Board
LT	London Transport
LTE	London Transport Executive
LU/LUL	London Underground/London Underground Limited
MPU	Motive Power Unit
MR	Metropolitan Railway
NET	Nottingham Express Transit
NTFL	New Tube for London
PTE	Passenger Transport Executive
SPT	Strathclyde Partnership for Transport
SSL	Sub-Surface Line
SYPTE	South Yorkshire Passenger Transport Executive
SYSL	South Yorkshire Supertram Limited
TfGM	Transport for Greater Manchester
TfL	Transport for London
tph	Trains per Hour
TRV	Track Recording Vehicle
W&C	Waterloo & City Line
W&CR	Waterloo & City Railway
WMCA	West Midlands Combined Authority

LIVERY CODES

AL	Advertising Livery
0	Other (non-standard) Livery

APPENDIX III. WEIGHTS & MEASUREMENTS

AC	Alternating current
Ah	Amp-hour
DC	Direct current
hp	Horsepower
kN	Kilonewtons
kW	Kilowatts
lbf	Pounds force
lbf/sq. in.	Pounds force per square inch
m	Metres
mm	Millimetres
mph	Miles per hour
tonnes	Metric tonnes
tons	Imperial tons
TOPS	Total Operations Processing System
V	Volts

APPENDIX IV. PRIVATE MANUFACTURERS

ABB	ASEA Brown Boveri, (later ABB, now Bombardier Transportation)
Adtranz	ABB/Daimler-Benz Transport
Alstom	Alstom Transportation
Ansaldo	AnsaldoBreda (now Hitachi Rail Italy)
AP	Aveling & Porter
BN	BN Construction (now Bombardier Transportation)
Bombardier	Bombardier Transportation
BP	Beyer Peacock and Company
BR	British Railways (later British Rail)
BRCW	Birmingham Railway Carriage & Wagon Company
BREL	British Rail Engineering Limited (later BREL, then ABB, now Bombardier Transportation)
Brush	Brush Traction
BTH	British Thomson-Houston Company
CAF	Construcciones y Auxiliar de Ferrocarriles
CL	Cammel Laird
Clayton	Clayton Equipment
Cowans	Cowans, Sheldon and Company
Cravens	Cravens Railway Carriage & Wagon Company
EE	English Electric Company
Firema	Firema Trasporti
GEC	General Electric Company (later GEC, then GEC-Alsthom, now Alstom)
GRCW	Gloucester Railway Carriage & Wagon Company
HB	Hunslet-Barclay Limited (now Wabtec Corporation)
Hunslet	Hunslet Engine Company (now Wabtec Corporation)
Hurst	Hurst Nelson & Company
Kawasaki	Kawasaki Rail Car, Inc
Mather	Mather & Platt
Matisa	Matisa Matériel Industriel SA
MC	Metropolitan-Cammell Carriage & Wagon Company (later Metro-Cammell)
MV	Metropolitan-Vickers
Neasden	Metropolitan Railway Neasden Works
Oldbury	Oldbury Railway Carriage & Wagon Company
Plasser	Plasser & Theurer
RFS	RFS Industries (now Wabtec Corporation)
RR	Rolls-Royce
Schoma	Christoph Schöttler Maschinenfabrik GmbH (now Schöma)
Siemens	Siemens AG
Stadler	Stadler Rail
VL	Vossloh Locomotives
Vossloh	Vossloh Rail Vehicles
Wickham	D Wickham and Company

▲ LUL Central Line trains 91223 (left) and 91169 (right) cross at East Acton on a glorious 22 May 2012.
Robert Pritchard

▼ New Stadler tram-train 399 207 is seen on test at Cathedral on 5 April 2017. These vehicles are due to enter service on the South Yorkshire Supertram system in 2017.
Tony Caddick

PLATFORM 5 MAIL ORDER

FROM GRIDIRON TO GRASSLAND
THE RISE AND FALL OF
BRITAIN'S RAILWAY
MARSHALLING YARDS

by Michael Rhodes

HARDBACK. £34.95

Over three decades of research by well-known railway author, Michael Rhodes, have produced this definitive history. It examines British Railways' policy towards marshalling yards in light of the 1955 Modernisation Plan and looks at individual yards in detail; from the earliest yards to the first mechanised hump yards, the Modernisation Plan yards and finally Britain's last, fully automated, hump yards. 288 pages with 500 photographs, 50 plans and 80,000 words. An invaluable reference book for anyone interested in Britain's railways.

Postage & packing : 10% UK; 20% Europe; 30% Rest of the World

PLATFORM 5 PUBLISHING LTD, 52 BROADFIELD ROAD, SHEFFIELD, S8 0X.
Mail Order Department 0114 255 8000